ADVANCED PSYCHIC DEVELOPMENT

Becky Walsh

First published by O Books, 2007
O Books is an imprint of John Hunt Publishing Ltd.,
The Bothy, Deershot Lodge, Park Lane, Ropley, Hants, SO24 0BE, UK
office1@o-books.net
www.o-books.net

Distribution in:

UK and Europe
Orca Book Services
orders@orcabookservices.co.uk
Tel: 01202 665432 Fax: 01202 666219 Int. code (44)

USA and Canada
NBN
custserv@nbnbooks.com
Tel: 1 800 462 6420 Fax: 1 800 338 4550

Australia and New Zealand
Brumby Books
sales@brumbybooks.com.au
Tel: 61 3 9761 5535 Fax: 61 3 9761 7095

Far East (offices in Singapore, Thailand, Hong Kong, Taiwan)
Pansing Distribution Pte Ltd
kemal@pansing.com
Tel: 65 6319 9939 Fax: 65 6462 5761

South Africa
Alternative Books
altbook@peterhyde.co.za
Tel: 021 447 5300 Fax: 021 447 1430

Design: Stuart Davies

ISBN: 978 1 84694 062 0

A CIP catalogue record for this book is available from the British Library.

Printed in the US by Maple Vail

ADVANCED PSYCHIC DEVELOPMENT

Becky Walsh

BOOKS

Winchester, UK
Washington, USA

CONTENTS

INTRODUCTION

The western world's perception of psychics and mediums is changing. Our new generation no longer sees them as gypsy fortune-tellers or ancient mystics. With this new wave of interest, we need a better understanding of what it is to be psychic and how the work of the psychic is changing.

This is the psychic's bible. It is a must for any budding or advanced psychic medium, anyone interested in a career as an energy-worker, and also a guide for everyone wishing to better understand and deepen their relationships with their loved ones. You don't need to want to become a psychic or a medium to benefit from this book, as the skills detailed in it can transfer to any relationship. These are not party tricks, they are life skills. By learning to unlock and use our innate intuitive ability, we can become better partners, parents, friends and work colleagues, enabling us to become better communicators, as well as better listeners, both verbal and non-verbal. Expanding psychic ability isn't just about becoming a psychic, whatever that means; it's about reaching your potential, getting in-tune with yourself and being the best person you can be.

However, as people become more comfortable with the idea of visiting a psychic or energy practitioner in order to resolve a personal issue, it is clear that this is a growth industry. Many are starting to see it as an acceptable choice for their career, being drawn to it for many reasons.

For example:

- They have always felt a desire to help people.
- The work is incredibly fulfilling and has a very sociable aspect.
- Psychics are getting media recognition, and many have become celebrities in their own right.
- The idea of having 'supernatural powers' is, for some, quite appealing.

- It can be an option for those seeking a career change, and has the advantages of not requiring mandatory testing or qualifications at present.
-

However, for anyone wishing to take that extra step and make a career of it, there are still many drawbacks.

- The term 'psychic' and what that means is hugely misunderstood both by the public, and even by psychics themselves, due to misleading information from 'psychics' of the past, and from those who would discredit them.
- This misunderstanding can sometimes leave psychics themselves confused as to what their job can or should be, not to mention lacking in confidence.
- Some people are so convinced that all psychics are charlatans that they feel justified in putting psychics down, even to the point of being abusive.
- There is, as yet, no psychic trade union and very little support and advice for people once they do start working professionally.
- The industry is unregulated and there is no officially recognised code of practice. As a result, there are horror stories where clients have been told things by psychics that have haunted them long after the reading.

This book works at different levels; from recognising your own psychic ability, to the real training that can take it further. When I say further, I mean beyond people's normal comprehension of what is possible to achieve in this physical dimension.

Is this book for you?

Many people are interested in what happens to the 'self' after you die. Do our personalities live on after death? And if so, are we held to account for our lives before some kind of judgement panel, who hold up score cards for what we did right and how much we got wrong? Then, are we given a kind of punishment for our wrongdoings, the penance for which could be seen as another lifetime?

It's at that point of full circle that I find to be the most interesting. I don't care much for what happens when I die. I trust myself to deal with it when I get there. In my mind, there is life after death. That being the case, when did I come into being? Did my existence start when I was born to this lifetime? As I believe in life after death, what about life before birth? I don't remember being a baby, or remember being in the womb as I only had a subconscious mind at that point, it is also then likely that I wouldn't remember being around before the womb. If this be the case, which I believe it is, why did I choose to be born? I must have chosen this, as we have free will. Why indeed did YOU choose to be born, at this time and in this space?

The fact that you are reading this book suggests to me that your reasoning is much the same as mine. We are born in this time and space to empower people (in much the same way as this book's aim is to empower its readers).

The world is going through a vibrational shift. Many people who are waking up to the idea that 'this physical world can't be all there is' are doing so for a reason. With the wars, the now obvious global warming, the natural disasters and the general state of the world, people are looking for spiritual answers. There is a growing sense that the answer can be found within us. Those of us who are waking up may all find different routes to the answer, and psychic development is one of the routes people are discovering.

Psychic development is a journey, and a far bigger one than learning to do a reading for someone, or recognising if a person at work finds you attractive. Many think that becoming psychic is the destination, and once psychic, you can use these so-called 'powers' any way you want to. But there comes a point when you realise it's a Pandora's box. Once opened, it is hard to close (not that you would want to). We need to grow and develop in order to get it right. But what is right? How do you know when you have finished? If we all became psychic would it change the world? The answer is yes! If we could all feel what others feel, there would be no separation, only a feeling of oneness. Therefore, what is happening to you is experienced by the whole. How, in other words, can we not help each other?

I have met many un-spiritual psychics, very gifted, but who have no awareness. They suffer from fear, which shows itself in many forms. This was very true of some psychics and mediums of the past who felt that their gifts made them special but were unable to share due to the conviction that if everyone could develop psychically then they would lose their status. We see this in many organised religions. It leads to fear and wars. In the world of the psychic it leads to mistrust and scepticism.

This book is designed to remedy this, acting as a mentor to open the door and let out the mystery. The problem lies in the fact that we psychics hardly ever talk to each other, barely circulating the information on what/how we practice. This is then further compounded by the lack of information available to the public; there are very few non-psychics who are able to fully understand what our work entails. In order not to create a divide between those who have the knowledge and those who don't, I have written this book in the same way as one would write a letter to a friend, offering a friendly line of communication and connection.

As this is an advanced psychic development book you might be wondering if you are 'advanced' enough to carry on reading. This is not a subject in which you can gain recognised qualifications. So how much do you need to know in order to begin?

This book is an exploration of the energy vibration changes you go through as a developing spiritual and psychic person. There are books on psychic development as well as books on contacting your spirit guides and angels, but in truth there is a large gap in between the two. Many people jump straight into trying to meet their guides, finding that they may fail on the first try and give up or, even worse, decide that their guides don't exist and that it's all nonsense. To be able to contact spirit you need to raise your vibration. This book is an advanced book as it will take you through the levels of vibration from psychic to being able to tune in to the Akashic records. These are the records that hold the information of your past lives, the lessons to be learned in this and future lives; they even hold information on your soul groups, the people you choose to be born with time, and time again, and why these people are here with you now. This information is valuable to you as you will be able to remove not only your own blocks but also those of your clients and friends. In effect, this book is a vibrational journey guide, one that every psychic takes if they want to improve the skill of benefiting other people with their gifts.

The people in your life mirror you. This is especially true of clients who often are mirror issues you have had in your own life and the people you draw into your life. However, when doing this work, you will always be one or two octaves above your clients, sometimes even one or two octaves above the other people in your life, which can leave you feeling like the odd one out. But it is important to bear in mind that it is the people in your life that keep you growing. We are all linked as one. You will find that you will meet people who are one or two octaves above you when you are on a growth spurt. However, your guides are always there to guide you into your next attunement stage.

This book is set into sound parts, giving the sound vibration for each level of development to help you become the best psychic possible. As your clients mirror you, we will also discuss the best ways of unblocking the clients and yourself at the vibrational level of that moment. Considering that such blocks occur in everyone throughout their lifetime to a greater or lesser degree, this book is intended for everyone, even if you don't see yourself as advanced. The fact that the book is in your hands is enough!

So this book isn't just for practitioners, it is for all people who want to develop on a deeper level and have a better understanding of themselves, and who want to help and empower others in a protected, safe way.

About the author

I haven't always known I was a psychic medium, but I've always known that people find me somewhat different. It is my aim to give everyone a positive perspective on what they see as different, to know it's not THAT different at all.

As far back as I can remember I have always felt like there was something I had to do, but I couldn't quite put my finger on it. When I look back over my life, I see patterns that now make me realise I am following my life's purpose, the work I decided to be born for. It is as if I looked from the spirit world at a war zone and decided to go into the heart of the conflict, trying to bring peace and healing. I haven't always chosen to do this in a passive manner. Many times I have gone in mouth blazing. Psychics aren't perfect; most of the best ones I've known have had difficult lives, it helps you empathise with other people in their difficulties. Looking back, I can see clearly how every decision that I made, (even the ones that I thought at the time were a failure or a waste of time) have lead me here, to right where I am meant to be. I still get angry or really fed up. I know I am physical and I enjoy having emotions of the ego and overcoming fears, but I live now as much as possible in alignment with myself, the universe and source energy (love).

I remember the time I first heard about readings and what they are. I was six or seven years old. I had gone to spend the summer at a friend's house without my family. My friend's mum, with whom I was staying, was a self-confessed Witch and even the kids on the estate where she lived called her a Witch to her face, to which she would say 'yes I am'. I found it really shocking and powerful at the same time. I was still trying hard to fit in and knew on many levels people found me strange. Being proud of being weird was something new to me.

My friend Rachel boasted of her mum's power telling me she

could see the future. It was then that I had my first reading. I may have forgotten most of my childhood, but I can still remember the reading. Rachel's mum told me I was going to live in America, marry an American, have two children and be an actress. She also said I had a toy dog that was magical, and I would know which one it was as it had a funny nose. I put great belief in what she told me and it was to be my first lesson in future prediction.

When I got home I went through my toys and found Puppy. Mum had sewn a nose onto Puppy using wool. This had to be who the psychic was talking about. I started to talk to Puppy until one day I could hear Puppy talking back, but the voice was in my mind. Later, I realised this was my spirit guide. From that first experience with Puppy, many different guides used different toys to talk to me, so much so that I felt that I didn't need to communicate with people that much. I enjoyed talking to spirit or rather, as I thought, my toys, much more. As I got older, I put the toys down and had direct communication with spirit. I don't remember analysing the change over, it simply was what I did.

I wasn't bright at school, and spent most of the time not listening to the teachers and daydreaming. Being dyslexic, I was put in the special needs group, which meant my art lessons were used for extra English and maths. I now know that my right brain, the creative side, is well developed, which helps in psychic ability. People with Asperger Syndrome have an advanced left brain, which can mean they have difficulty with emotion and empathy but may also be brilliant at maths and memory. I didn't pass a maths exam but I do have an amazing understanding of people. This is just the difference between the left and right brain.

Having developed an interest in psychic readings from the age of seven, it wasn't until I was a teenager that I was able to delve into the subject. I went to local psychic fairs thinking that if I touched a psychic they would know things about me. I didn't give any psychic eye contact as I walked round the tables. One lady said, 'I can see something about you.' 'What?' I asked. 'Give me some money and I'll tell you,' she replied.

Most of the psychics were old and looked like they were deeply unhappy. The energy in their rooms was desperate and dark. I saw a few public demonstrations. I really wanted to have this 'gift'. I thought to be psychic you had to have amazing powers not many others possessed; to be old, wear purple clothes and be festooned with crystals. It wasn't a very attractive thought. I also wanted to fit in with the norm, and these people didn't seem normal. They looked weird and had a funny energy around them. I didn't know at the time that I might have been able to sit at one of those tables even then and do readings.

But I now had an interest in trying to do readings for friends. At the time I was looking for the wrong evidence that I was psychic. I was looking to tell people facts I couldn't have known and to predict the future. When the information was hit and miss, as it would be, I thought the hits were luck. So I didn't think I was psychic, despite being able to tune into people's thoughts and feelings. This I thought everyone could do, not realising that not everyone can do this to the same level.

When I was in my early twenties, I was studying stage management and working on a fringe show in Camden called 'Big Buddha Beach'. One of the actresses in the show pulled me aside and said, 'Now I know why I am on this bloody show! I am meant to meet you.' I became very excited for not only did she tell me that she was psychic, but she was young, attractive and looked normal! She told me that I was a medium and must come round to her house for a reading. The reading she gave me was rubbish, but during it there was a knock at the door. A man came in, who was overjoyed to see me. She told me he was a fellow of the Spiritualist Association of Great Britain otherwise known as the SAGB. He went on to say that I was the most powerful natural medium he had ever met. He then invited me to a visitation ceremony.

Two days later the actress called me to say that this man was possessed and wanted to change bodies. That closed the door on working with other people for me, and even made me doubt that I was right to be a psychic. It also put me off the SAGB, which is a shame as many brilliant mediums have worked there.

I then spent time developing on my own, always having communication with my guides who taught me directly via life experience. Twenty years ago, there weren't the books available that there are now.

When I finally became fed up with working in theatre, having hit a block on the career ladder because of my dyslexia, I asked my guides what they thought I should do. Being dyslexic I felt my options were limited and I had already tried being a stand-up comic, a radio presenter and an actress. The guides said I could work with them and help people. That meant becoming a purple-wearing weirdo-psychic. One of my concerns that I told spirit was that this would halve my opportunities to meet someone and have a relationship. In response they sent me an understanding boyfriend whose mum was a psychic and whose dad was a healer. Thanks to that support, I was able to develop very quickly.

When I first started giving readings, I was working as a stage manager on cruise ships. There I discovered I could hear people in the spirit world. In-between ship contacts and theatre work, I started my education at the *College of Psychic Studies,* where I now teach foundation, intermediate and advanced psychic development. I continued to spend my evenings in the theatre and my days doing readings, hiring a small round room in the Phoenix Theatre, where the show *Blood Brothers* was running.

After a period of about 12 years, I finally gave up the theatre work and worked full time as a psychic medium. To begin with, this meant sitting in a shop called *Watkins* in London, waiting for someone to come in for a reading which meant spending most of the day earning no money. Quickly the word spread about my work and I started running workshops on psychic development. Now I enjoy an amazing life, one I never dreamt I would achieve. I'm a radio show presenter of the *Psychic Show* on LBC 97.3fm, I write for magazines, I am fully booked with readings, and I make appearances on TV. I also give talks and run workshops in a multitude of venues and festivals. Despite these joyous and fulfilling opportunities, I would like to add that there are still occasions when I sit on my sofa having a cry about the pressures of life!

The number one thing I love about this work is being able to live my life's purpose in empowering people, changing the world into a better place in whichever way possible, no matter how small. These changes can be manifested even for the lady on the bus who strikes up a conversation with me and I am able to say what she needs in that moment; or for my friends, family and valued clients, an ability from which they have always benefited. Over the years, as my vibration and my work has developed, the types of clients and friends coming into my life have changed. I have gone from clients wanting future predictions and facts about relationships to ones who say, 'I don't know why I'm here, I just felt drawn to come.' In my friendships I have gone from people who need something from me, to people I get to share with. As you will start to recognise in this book, the more you range your own sound vibration, the more you can tune into others' songs. The faces I remember, the names I forget.

I hope this book helps you to find your own life's purpose.

PART ONE

TUNING UP THE PSYCHIC VIBRATION

We live in a technological age, defining ourselves through matter rather than spirit. We tend to think: 'If I have this and own that, then I am successful; if I am successful, then I am a good person and I will be respected and loved.' We measure whether we're sad or happy by what we own.

But it doesn't satisfy us. We're always looking for something else. Say, for example, you're at work in an office. There is a mountain of paper to get through, you are fed up and want to go home, but then you remember that in your back pocket is a ticket for a trip to the Caribbean, and tomorrow you will be on that long-awaited flight. A large smile comes over your face. The work hasn't gone away, your current situation is still the same, but only now are you happy. Fast forward to the last day of your holiday – you remember you have to go to work the next day, and misery descends, even though you're lying on a sun-drenched beach.

Happiness is a question of perspective. When we believe that things outside ourselves make us happy, then we keep our minds busy with those things. Our culture, as a whole, believes that if we can have the right things around us, control our surroundings, then we will be happy. But controlling our surroundings for our own benefit is generally at the expense of someone else. With the way the world is going, with natural disasters, wars and global warming, more and more people are waking up to the fact that this control we are fighting to have is, in fact, an illusion. The world needs to change, but the change can only come from people who recognise their responsibility for what they have been given in terms of the foundation for future generations.

How do we change the world? Most attempts, however well-meaning, are frustrated because they still focus on trying to change the surroundings. Whenever we do that, we meet resistance. There is another way to change the world, and it starts with us. It's the psychic's way.

The psychic begins with changing spirit rather than matter. This way works because, ultimately, all matter is spirit. Everything that exists is simply a different form of the same thing: vibrating energy.

It is now generally accepted that all physical matter is made up of atoms. Within the atom exist smaller 'particles' – protons, neutrons and electrons – more easily understood as pure energy, little particles or waves of energy in vibration separated by large distances of space. At this ***quantum*** level of existence, everything consists of tiny packets of energy, and empty space. 99.9999% of an atom is empty space.

Energy itself, according to Albert Einstein in his formula $E=MC^2$, is mass (M) multiplied by the speed of light (C) squared. Depending on the way the energy is structured determines the frequency at which it *vibrates*. So, the metal that makes up a hammer is energy vibrating in such a way that, from our perspective and relative to our own vibration, it appears heavy, dense and solid. Yet it is no more solid than a hammer in a dream. In fact, nothing that we believe to be solid is truly solid. We just perceive it that way. In the real world, nothing is permanent. The only constant is continuous movement and change. The same is true of our emotions. They are also moving, vibrating and changing, made up of tiny chemical particles. You might feel fear in the pit of your stomach, or joy and love in your heart.

So what does this have to do with being psychic? There is now a scientific term for psychic ability, *Anomalous Cognition* (or AC. The transfer of information through means other than the 5 traditional senses). Many within the scientific community are increasingly ready to accept these ideas, if not publicly then certainly in private. Maybe one day we can call ourselves AC practitioners. It would be wonderful to leave the name psychic in the past with 'Madam Ruth' and the fortune-tellers.

A psychic is aware of his/her energy, of the frequency at which it vibrates. They can change it, adapting it to be in sync with someone else, or the energy of an object or environment. For example, if you are in a good mood, and you take a seat on a coach and find your mood quickly shifting to something less pleasant, you will know if this is 'you', or if you have picked up on the vibration of the person who just stepped out of the seat, or indeed the collective energy of the people on the bus.

It's like the keys on a piano being tuned to the right pitch with each other. We blend our energy with the energy around us. That is why we feel relaxed in the countryside. It is a slower pace of life, and why many people in the country don't like 'city folk'. We arrive in the country still vibrating quickly, and it takes us time to 'wind down'.

At present a shift in consciousness has started, moving from the material to the spiritual. This involves a shift in vibration. We are living through a spiritual revolution in which people are becoming increasingly aware that if you don't look within yourself for answers, you end up with no answer at all. Becoming an advanced psychic means taking part in this revolution. It means you also need to be an advanced spiritual person as the two go hand in hand. If you don't have one, the other won't work for you. You can't be a person who has jealousy in your heart and be able to help someone become everything they ever dreamed they could be. But it has nothing to do with extra-ordinary or unnatural powers. *Any* person can learn to develop psychic ability. We mostly had it as young children, but social conditioning drummed it out of us. It is what you now do with this ability that makes you special. To be psychic is to be in tune with energy, be aware of it and be able to make use of it in order to help others as well as yourself.

However, being a psychic is not the same as being a medium. Mediums have developed the ability to communicate through the medium of mind. They can contact the spirits of those in other dimensions of space and time, including that which we commonly call 'the afterlife'. They are in-between two or more worlds. We will look at this later.

A stage further from being a medium is channelling. To channel is to allow a spirit guide or ascended master to speak directly through you. This is sometimes done unconsciously. Here, the medium's imagination doesn't get in the way of the information coming from spirit, and can't edit it. Often the medium won't even remember what was said.

Further on still, there is communication from the angelic realms. This usually takes the form of healing, of releasing fear and imparting love, rather than information or facts. It can take place in a reading without the client even being aware it is happening. Often the lessons are hard to accept, but the angelic energy makes the pill easier to swallow as contact with the angelic realm enables you to see yourself lovingly, as an aspect of God, rather than taking the blame for your troubles.

Next we move to the Akashic records. The best way to understand this is to think of a library with books describing everything that has gone before and everything that will be. At this level of vibration you can see the past and the future. It may be for your own benefit, for your own evolution, or for those around you. Alternatively, you may travel the time lines, also known as shamanic journeying, a form of meditation/visualisation. We may think of time lines in terms of forward and back, but time is as much an illusion of physical world as solidity, it doesn't really exist. Time lines are all around us, the matrix through which we move. Through visualisation you can 'intend' what you want to see based on what you are doing. Perhaps you want to unblock an issue in your current life. You can find its origins in a past life, look into the future to see how you will benefit from releasing it, and use the future as a form of encouragement.

Moving on from this, we finally get to the level of God's creative energy. This creative energy is hidden in all of us, even in our thoughts, and while it is something we have access to, few of us can cope with the responsibility that comes with it. Its finest expression is to help others find the God-creative force inside themselves, rather than interfere with their own life patterns.

So to be 'psychic' is a general term to describe a state of heightened awareness and receptivity, whereas to be 'advanced' is to begin the search for wisdom and enlightenment, trusting your own intuition and being in service to the truth. It means developing your sensitivity to subtle energy and the information that it carries.

The chakras

So how do we heighten our awareness and receptivity? By changing our vibration to become more sensitive to the energy of others. One way to do this is to open the chakras.

The word *chakra* comes from Sanskrit and means 'wheel'. Chakras are known as centres, or *wheels,* of energy located on the midline of the body supplying much of the colour and energy of the aura. There are seven main chakras and they each have different colours associated with them, representing different aspects or levels of the self.

When the subtle energy levels of the chakras are in harmony then the physical body maintains an equilibrium and a positive relationship between the mental, emotional and spiritual bodies.

As an advanced psychic development student, I would expect you to have an understanding of the chakras and so this information will not be covered in depth. If you feel the need to know more on chakras there are many books on the market that cover purely the energy centres themselves.

1 - Root chakra, also called base/kundalini - red

The root chakra is about grounding and feeling connected to the earth, solid and strong in all situations. This chakra is linked with sexual energy.

2 - Sacral chakra - orange

The sacral chakra is about feeling and emotion.

3 – Solar plexus chakra - yellow

The solar plexus chakra helps you pick up others' energy. You may have a feeling that you need to cross the road as someone is walking towards you; this is likely to be a warning from the solar plexus. It stands out in front of the body and brings back information about people. You may be picking up other people's energy and be working like a psychic sponge if this is a very active chakra for you.

4 - Heart chakra - green

The heart chakra is about love.

5 - Throat chakra - blue

The throat chakra is about self-expression and talking.

6 - Third eye chakra - violet

The third eye chakra is about insight and visualisation. When it is open and working, you have a good intuition. If it is under-active, you're not very good at thinking for yourself and you may tend to rely on authorities. You might even get confused easily. If this chakra is over-active then you may live in a world of fantasy.

7 - Crown chakra - white

The crown chakra is your connection to the spirit world.

As well as the seven main chakras there are minor chakras on the palms and on the soles of the feet. Invisible energy lines known as meridians connect all the chakras. Meridians, like the veins and arteries which carry our blood, are channels of energy that run through the body.

Grounding

Grounding is a word often used when we do any psychic work and I believe it's vital to be grounded after a psychic session, but not so important during. It is important, however, to be centred during a session, and this is a subject we shall talk more about later. For the moment it is enough to know that grounding is the feeling of connectedness to the earth, our bodies and to the present moment. We are our consciousness, and we are wherever our thoughts are or where our *attention* is. A lot of the time our thoughts are not 'grounded' in the present. Our attention travels to the past, to the future, to different places and people. We find ourselves daydreaming and saying things like, 'sorry, I was miles away.' You literally were. Sometimes it is necessary to bring your attention back to where your physical body is. This is very true after giving a reading or experiencing a moment of inspiration. Sometimes we can feel disconnected from ourselves, sometimes even leading to possibly dangerous situations – myself having been nearly hit by a car when crossing the road, as a result of not being present in my body.

There are certain activities that naturally ground us. Dancing, cooking, cleaning, gardening, eating, making love, walking in nature and playing with a pet are all activities that have the effect of grounding us. From an energetic point of view, grounding can be likened to the earth wire in an electric circuit. It has the positive effect of re-balancing us, putting us back into our bodies, and into the present.

If, for some reason, we forget to ground, or have a personality which likes to live in our minds instead of our bodies, then we may experience a lack of clarity and focus, or increased stress levels and decreased ability to cope with that stress.

Exercise: Basic chakra meditation

Sit, with your back straight on a straight backed chair. Choose a time when you will not be disturbed for this process.

Rest your hands lightly on your lap, thighs or knees, with your palms up.

Take a moment to focus your attention on your breathing; make sure it is soft and regular and you are in the most relaxed space you can be.

When you are ready, imagine sending roots down from your feet, though the floor, through the foundations of the building and right the way down into the earth. Let these roots travel until they get to a natural end, and when they do, make an anchor from them. Know that you are safe and grounded in your connection to the earth.

Feel the earth's energy, rising up through those roots as you breathe. You can see this as a red colour or light, if you like. Feel it as the energy coming up through the roots, up though your feet, up your legs and up to the base chakra, feeling that bright red energy open up before you. You can see this as a flower opening or a bright light being switched on.

Pull the energy up to the sacral chakra, which now opens up orange before you in the same way.

Breathe the energy up again to the solar plexus which is a bright yellow energy standing out from your body in the centre of your chest.

Send the energy up to your heart chakra which is a green energy (some say with a hint of pink).

Breathe the energy up again to the throat chakra, which is a turquoise blue opening up before you.

Breathe the energy up again to your third eye and see the eye opening with a beautiful violet colour.

Breathe the energy up again to connect with the crown chakra in a display of bright white energy. Know that this is connecting to the spirit world which is above you and all around, surrounding you.

Take a moment to sit in that energy, your own energy and experience what this feels like.

When you are ready, open your eyes. Have a look around you. Does the room seem brighter, more colourful?

It is important to note your own energy in the same way at different times in the day with as many different things as you are doing. Once you know what you feel like, you will know the difference between you and anything else that comes into your energy field.

Closing the chakras

When the chakras are open, the energy feels great. But if we walk around in everyday life like this, it makes it easy to pick up negativity or rather, as I would like to call it, 'dense energy'. It is really important that you 'close down' these centres each time you have finished any psychic work or finished exercising in this way. This gives a sense of discipline. It lets spirit know when you are working, and gives you a way to clock in and clock out of work. On a subtle level we are all aware of people's energy. Being open can also mean you are open to others who can milk your energy.

Just as you have visualised the energy moving up through your body, opening up the chakra centres, visualise going back down, seeing the petals close, or seeing the colours as lights being dimmed and switched off. You can even imagine doors on the centres closing.

Ways to tune up vibration

It is possible to stay at a high frequency of vibration and not lose your energy to others. This is to be at a high frequency, but not open and receptive. Think of people like Mother Teresa or the Dalai Lama.

Some emotions are dense vibrations, which greatly influence our lives. Fear is a dense vibration, and our aim is to live without fear, replacing it with love. We can only achieve this by working through our individual fears. We were not born fearful. We originally looked at certain aspects of life and decided that 'this is bad, because it feels bad'. We need to re-decide many of those decisions by recognising that something is dark only because we have decided it is so. If we see everything as light, it will bring us to a light vibration, something more akin to spirit – what you might call heaven vibration on earth.

See inspiration in everything. It's easy to pay attention to how bad things can be. Look at the beauty in everything and make time to do so. How can you help other people rise out of their perspective or darkness if you share that darkness with them? The world is full of the most amazing things. If you find yourself being a glass-half-empty person, keep a pillow book. Every night write down the things about the day that you are grateful for or happy about, highlighting a new favourite discovery, be that a person or something someone said, a term you have never heard before. It's important to be a positive person as this is the energy you will pass into the world as well as your clients.

We get so used to the way the world is we forget to look for something new. Some time ago, I took my dog for a walk in a different park to normal and noticed her looking up at a tree with great wonder. At this point she was only six months old. I thought to myself how wonderful it would be to find something as simple as a tree to be as amazing as the look on her face. It took a moment to realise she was listening to the birds in the tree and I looked up to find thirty or more birds eating from pods on the branches. These birds were green parrots. Green parrots on Dulwich Common in London! We miss the exotic when we keep our eyes on the ground.

How the brain reserves psychic information.

It seems to me that when we are children we are praised for performing mental skills, such as remembering you times table in Maths or solving logic problems. These are skills that can be measured through exams. There has never been an exam in common sense as it isn't something you can measure. But if you were to employ someone with out common sense you could measure it in financial loss!

This is also true of intuition, it can't be measured. Yet some of the most successful businesses started with someone having a hunch or an intuitive thought for an idea or and investment. Having learnt in school that you only get rewarded for answering questions that you could figure out the answer, we don't value our gut intuition as it simply doesn't reap the same rewards in attention and praise from teachers.

The brain has a distinct difference between its left and right hemisphere as the two sides function independently of each other. The left side can do your home work whilst the right side is listening to music.

The left hemisphere is considered dominant as it is the centre of language.

The right is none verbal, it cannot keep time or space but it can create and move mental images such as clairvoyant images. The left side perceives information in steps and pieces, the right perceives as a whole.

This explains how when a left brain person likes a motor bike they will think of the power of the engine. They might want to know about the breaks and the fairings.

A right brain person will look at the shape and the colour. This explains the age joke about women and cars. They choose a car by the colour and not much else. Feminine energy is predominantly right brain.

The left brain sees the motor bike in parts, the right brain as a whole.

But the gith brain lack the language to explain the bike. So it send the picture to the left brain who interprets it and puts it into words. Or the right brain might send a signal to the limbic system, which will send a physical sensation or anemotion.

All psychic information goes to the right brain.

Which is why when giving a reading information comes to the right brain from spirit or you intuition or one of the many other Clare senses. You then need to allow the left brain to communicate it. Most tests for psychics and mediums are left brain tests. You can't test the right brain with a left brain test. It also explains why sometimes the person receiving the reading can't understand what you are talking about. You might as a psychic misunderstand ansity for excitment. A simple error to make when crossing from one side of the mind to the other.

It would help to think of it as My rational, logical mind thinks this way and my intuitive mind sees it that way'.

As a dyslexic I have a stronger right mind, which means that all the left brain education I was given at school was lost on me.

What's the difference between Intuitive and Psychic ability?

Intuition is the sum total of everything that we've experienced in a life time, and stored in the unconscious processes.

Psychic is a word most people put in connection with mysterious and supernatural connections. Its true meaning is 'beyond known physical processes'. You can see why intuition might get mistaken for psychic ability. Both Psychic and intuition feel the same to the person receiving the information or feeling.

It is understood that the best psychic have had very full lives. I believe this is because they have more to draw from in the intuition, as intuition is the sub total of all of our live experiences. How ever if you had a client who was going in a relationship with a lead singer in a famous band, and in your life you had your heart broken by the lead singer of a famous band who painfully left you for another person. You might have an intuitive insight based on your own past and predict for your client that there relationship will end with the same fait. Of course this doesn't happen to be true, what happened to you might not happen to another. But with your whole faith in your psychic ability you wouldn't realise where this information was coming from.

The really sad part is you could then cause the break up of that relationship. Your client would then start acting mistrust of her partner, and a cause and effect situation would cause them to break up.

This is one of the many reasons why I don't believe that prediction the future is a positive thing to do.

It really is impossible to tell 100% between psychic and intuitive information.

As many of your clients will go through similar life experiences to your own, it is valid to draw from your own life when giving advice. But do send out a little question to spirit if you are in any doubt about where your information is coming from. Often spirit will interrupt the reading if you are going down the wrong track, but letting you know that this information is only relevant to you.

You will get this in a form of 'just knowing' you are on the wrong track. Don't feel embarrassed to correct something you have said just after you have said it.

During a reading you just the best you can.

The personality

The word 'personality' comes from the Greek word *per-sona*, meaning 'through sound', personality being the expression of ourselves through sound.

Our true Selves somehow lie behind the face we show to the world, namely our personality, whereas our voice, or the sounds we make, reveals the truth of who we are, our inner self as such.

However, sound is synonymous with vibration, which means that everything that exists is made of vibrating energy. Therefore everything is, in turn, made of sound.

Hence, literally being a good and nice person tunes up your vibration. The most powerful thing is being true to your word in that you should never say anything that you don't mean or won't stand by. By becoming completely true to your word you are giving people the feeling they can trust you, which in itself is, of course, an important part of being a great psychic.

This truth and integrity to your word must be validated in every area of your life. For example, never say to someone I'll see you at six o'clock and then be five minutes late. This is a hard thing to stick to, but you can use the wording 'I intend to see you at six o'clock'. That way you can't let anybody down. This goes for your written words too as people seem to see the power in the written word more than in that which is spoken.

Becoming more powerful as a psychic means becoming more powerful as a person, and in turn being able to bring your words into creation with more strength and force. Never speaking ill of others or yourself will help improve your vibrational level, because every time we see the world and other people as less than perfect, we end up lowering our vibration. In effect, we focus on the problem without creating the solution.

Judgement

Why do we judge others? To make them wrong so we can feel right; to make them the bad ones so we can feel like the good ones. Yet whenever we judge another we are judging and blocking ourselves. Imagine that within you is every possible potential version of you, the hero, the murderer, the healer, the thief, the comedian, the manipulator – all these aspects of you you may not like. Some of these aspects. You may prefer not to bring these particular potentials into your everyday reality because you understand the effects of doing so, and those particular effects you prefer to avoid. Some of these sides may only come out in response to very extreme circumstances. For example, it may take a threat upon the lives of our loved ones to bring out the aspect which would be willing to take a life.

We refuse to own these aspects of ourselves and try to place them as far away from our sense of identity as we can, and we do this by making them the characteristics of someone else. We literally demonise another human being when we judge them as bad. 'I'm not that thing, that bad thing,' we say, 'I'm this good thing. It is him over there doing the bad thing who is wrong. It's his fault.' That which we see in them as bad, however, must be within us too, or we would not be able to recognise it.

Judgement is based on the ideas of absolutes like right and wrong. When we judge another and condemn them we are actually judging and condemning a part of ourselves, with every judgement making our world a little smaller.

We don't just judge people, we judge everything, from films, to cleaning, to ice-cream. We are expected to show good judgement in our lives, often making decisions based on the word 'should'. *Should I be doing this?* Our society is geared up to this way of thinking. We have the option between a right and a wrong decision, but in truth there is no such thing as a right or a wrong decision, for there is only judgement, often based on hindsight, that makes it so.

There are no right or wrong parts of our personality, for it is the intention behind an action which makes it either positive or negative. If I hit a person hard on the back for blocking my way, simply because I wanted to move faster than they were walking, then that would be unreasonable. However, if I punch someone who is choking on food, in order to save their life, then my action is coming from a loving place.

It's often feared that people will walk all over you if you are always coming from a place of understanding and thinking of others. Practicing non-judgement does not mean we have to tolerate abusive or selfish behaviour from others. In fact, if we allow others to abuse us or do things that we feel are unfair, then we deny our truth and in doing so abuse the abuser.

We don't have to make them wrong for what they are doing, we just let them know that their intentions towards us are unacceptable. They may subsequently repeat the same abusive patterns with other people in different situations. If it is our choice to serve, then we must serve the greater good, not the individual ego. The way to serve the world is to be in balance with yourself. This may sound like a contradiction, but you can only serve if the self is as whole and balanced as possible. The way to be in balance is to always come from the best of your self at all times, by making decisions and actions in the higher self and not from a place of fear. Practicing true non-judgement is just holding the intention that you will not consider someone as wrong or bad, and allowing yourself to recognise that it is not an individual person but their *intentions* that are out of alignment.

It is one of the hardest things to live without judgement, as the first thing you do when you make a judgement is to judge yourself for being judgmental. We then proceed to beat ourselves up for making the judgement and recommence the cycle of rights and wrongs, which leads right back to the word 'should'. If we allow things to just be, and release the idea of the outcome, we can find ourselves in a state of bliss where we are truly living in the moment, in a state of unity with the universe and with all life.

To aim to live without judgement is enough. You will find that others around you will also stop judging you. Most of us protect ourselves by sending out a judgement to the others judging us. As they say, 'behaviour breeds behaviour'. It has to stop somewhere and can stop with you. You can see judgement as dense energy that doesn't resonate with your life experience, that way you won't accept other judgements of you – very important for psychic work!

The law of creative thinking

Every thought and every act is creative. You will draw to you what you think is your reality. Create your own reality from your highest intention, and not from your greatest fear.

Whilst you cannot control your emotions, it is possible to control your thoughts, like the ones we have about ourselves and others. For example, if you are thinking on a negative, just literally *think again*. Ask: 'What would love do in this situation?' or 'What would love say to this thought?'

Everyone has an inner critic which points out ways you could improve yourself. What happens when this inner critic gets too much attention? It makes its job bigger. We start to get into a cyclic pattern of negative thinking. When we are thinking of something positive, we call it daydreaming, when we think of something negative, it's called preparation. When we think the negative over and over, it's called worrying. Worry and negative thoughts about ourselves tend to run in circles. The faster the cycle of thought is going, the greater the chance of bringing it into real life, due to the magnetism of the vibration of the thoughts spinning in our head. This includes thoughts such as 'I am an idiot', or 'this is going to go wrong', or 'I can't do it…'

We are aspects of God, and all of our thoughts have creative power, so when the wheel of words is buzzing around in your head, just STOP and think again. It doesn't matter if you think of pink fluffy clouds, as long as you stop the cycle.

The mind can be trained like a muscle to think on a positive level. You have 17 seconds to turn a negative thought into a positive one, before the negative thought turns into negative realisation. This is a very good exercise to teach your clients and friends, with the idea of making the world a better place. This discipline will also advance your psychic ability, because the mind and belief of what is possible can limit what you can achieve.

The law of resonance

All levels of the body respond to change in any one level through the law of resonance. If you wish to change how you feel, sometimes something as simple as changing your posture can be tremendously effective, especially since some ways of holding your body and of breathing create the ideal home for lower vibrational emotions. By correcting your posture and, more importantly, your breathing, you can create different and more positive feelings within your body. By consciously avoiding negativity in mind and body, you will find you have more control over your life, and you will attract more people to you that you have the energy to help.

Eating and drinking

Finally, another way to help you keep on a high level of vibration is to monitor what goes into your body! You are what you eat!

As everything has a vibrational energy, so does food and drink. It is only fair that, before I write a worthy list of good food to eat, I should let you know that I have a terrible diet! Yet I can still do the work of a psychic medium. This is advice for those who want to be limitless.

Many psychics experience carbohydrate and sugar cravings. These foods are very grounding – the body knows what will bring the spirit back to the body. They are also comfort foods that you will find you really need after meetings with some people!

It is a known fact that after a reading involving a lot of dense energy, some of that energy is absorbed by the psychic. Amazingly, this energy can be removed from the psychic by yawning! Before I realised this, I would crave coffee, thinking I was tired. The trick is to never stifle a yawn. These yawns are not small, they are the big jaw-breakers that make your eyes water. The problem is that when you need this yawn, it's often after the negative client has gone and the new client is sitting in front of you, wondering if they are boring you. You can't say, 'Sorry, but the last client was a real misery!' So I would say take a 15-minute break in between clients to room cleanse, cleanse yourself and have a few good yawns. We will talk more about cleansing later.

Eat a good percentage of raw fruits and vegetables (preferably organic) and new shoots and sprouts as they are very good for your vibration. If you eat meat, you are digesting the vibration of the emotion in the animal as it lived and died. Animals that have been brought up with a great life and didn't suffer when they died will be vibrationally more positive. All of the normal things we are nagged about when it comes to taking better care of ourselves apply to our energy and vibration.

Drugs make holes in the aura, damaging much more than just the body. I wouldn't advise anyone who is using drugs to develop psychically, even when using so called 'spiritual' drugs, such as

'Ayahuasca', which has been used as a way of connecting with other dimensions. Drugs change your vision of the world. You can believe that you are now seeing the world the way it really is in truth, but it is still only a variation of the matrix of life you are in; it is still the chemicals which exist in your physical body that the drugs are using to give you the experience.

Alcohol is also dense energy and, even though it is a legal drug, it isn't any better than other drugs. However, the personal intention can be different. Sharing a bottle of wine with friends has a different energy to wanting to have a hedonistic experience. The intention of personal abuse isn't the same. There is also intention of world abuse with drugs. In the city, it's hard to understand how the same people who buy fair trade products and eat organic food can be sniffing cocaine on the weekend without any thought of the deaths caused by drugs, or the harm to the environment.

Being spiritual is taking responsibility all of the time, for every action, even the long-term or out-of-sight results of your actions. This is the most positive way to be in alignment and start to raise your vibration.

Please understand that there is no fast way to vibration tuning. It is in everything you do and in every intention. It takes years to uncover our blocks, but that is the joy of it. It is a journey of self-discovery.

Energy protection

We have talked about how to raise your vibrational frequency, but how can you stop it from being lowered through the influence of other people and environments?

Most of us see ourselves as strong and independent in mind and body, yet we rely on each other for everything. We simply cannot live without each other. We are even linked by energy cords that run between us, our loved ones, work colleagues, even the person sitting next to us on the bus! It is impossible not to be connected by these energy cords, and therefore be linked to everyone in the world.

So when one suffers, in a diluted way we all suffer. Yet we continue to throw negative energy towards each other in the form of blame, jealousy and hate. I myself, whilst travelling on London Underground, have become annoyed with the person blocking the way on the other side of the ticket gate, feeling my entire energy lunge forward, silently screaming, '*get out of MY way*!' But we don't have our own way; it's just the space in front of us.

As the energy cords come out of the solar plexus area, you might feel a tug in that area at the end of a relationship or at the death of someone you know. After a connection with a person has passed, the cords will eventually wither and fall away; but new cords can grow, even in circumstances as simple as sleeping in the same bed as a person, or lending a listening ear.

How we can become drained or dense in vibration?

Anyone who has been to see a friend who is unwell may have noticed him/herself feeling tired and drained after seeing them. This is because we don't notice the energy of healing that we send them. In fact, it is also possible to feel this draining through normal everyday conversation, especially if someone is having a good old moan. One of the reasons we feel great after talking about our problems is that we have taken on board some of the listener's energy.

Exercise: The grape and the raisin

You can test this theory quite simply with a raisin, a grape and a sheet of white paper. Put the raisin and the grape onto a sheet of white paper about an inch apart. Relax your eyes and focus on the space between them. You should begin to become aware of the aura around the grape and the raisin. After some time you will notice something strange happening – auric energy will actually flow from the healthy grape to the dried grape, healing the raisin. This is exactly what happens when we give our energy to other people.

Attention and energy direction

Remember, where your attention goes, so does your energy. When you understand these energy mechanics you will start to notice all the situations where people help themselves to your energy, usually without being aware of it. The art is in learning to spot where your energy goes so that you can choose only to give of your energy where it is appropriate and of some use, thereby reclaiming your power and control. The saying 'letting things go' is really about not sending your attention to a place where you don't want to give your energy.

Fear is the greatest enemy

When talking about psychic protection, the last thing needed is to create fear as to why we would need protecting in the first place. What is it that we need protection from? What is out to get us? The truth is nothing that most of us haven't experienced in our life already.

Feeling that something is wrong on a psychic level needs careful examination.

First of all, you must carefully establish whether there is no ordinary explanation for your feelings. This will be made easier if you already know what your own energy feels like. Check that anything you are experiencing is not related in any way to recent stress or problems in your ordinary life, as stress is often the underlying cause of most 'reported' phenomena. It has been noted that once the stress or effects of recent trauma in a person's life have died down, so the psychic phenomena disappears!

Psychic attack

At some point in almost every day, we will come across someone else's negative thoughts and feelings, technically known as *psychic attack*. Whenever we have wished another ill, we have been guilty of psychic attack.

I see many clients who feel they have been cursed, or who believe that the hate of another person is making them ill. In one way they may be right, but in other ways it is their attachment to the problem that is making them believe that every negative thing that happens to them, down to missing the bus, is because of this negative energy. The trick is to put their fears into perspective and give them forms of protection they can use. This is a particularly important point to remember when dealing with people who feel that they are having an unjust life!

One of my students asked how she could protect herself from other peoples' energy on a crowded tube train. Information I was given from spirit is this 'If you are in a situation when you can't avoid other energy, be the energy you would like to feel in that situation. When you feel that the energy is negative you are adding to the negative energy with thoughts about your situation. You can transform the experience of the whole carriage by thinking, 'I am in this space to heal the space'. That way when you send out love in a situation where you feel discomfort and fear, you are changing the situation for many people including yourself.'

If a person is 'plugged into' the belief that there is lack in the world, all sorts of fears can occur, especially the idea that someone can take from them what they have, or that someone else will gain something that is meant for them. What is yours will not pass you by. Often because believe they could lose out to others, they fight for what they believe is their right, which in turn sends round a negative energy. Those who are sensitive may feel this, and people who are looking for a negative energy will also attach to this idea. When I first started on the radio show people kept telling me I was under attack from jealous people, and that I had to go for healing. Healers were telling friends of mine that they had tuned into me whilst I was on air, and they had picked up problems coming at me in the form of psychic attack; I was told that I must go for healing to be cleared. Over the period of a month I started to feel more and more drained, so I began looking at who might be sending me this attack. I tuned in during the show to see what was out there; it was like lying in bed trying to hear if someone has broken into the house. I asked Spirit for guidance as every little piece of bad timing was now starting to be attributed to this attack, and the next day someone phoned me to tell me again that they were worried about me. As they did so, Spirit showed me that the damage was coming from me buying into the possibility that my energy frequency had been weakened. I realised that it was my belief that this was possible which had created the problem. The minute I changed my state of mind and started to tell people it wasn't possible for me to be attacked, I felt better. My energy was restored and my fear disappeared. Although these well-intentioned people were the cause of the problem, I encouraged it too, by buying into their fear.

Negative spirits and demons

Again this is a difficult one. Like attracts like, so if you are a good person it's unlikely that you will come across anything negative. But being aware of negative entities means you can bring them into your life, simply by your awareness of them. This is known as the 'attraction of attention'. The trick is to have awareness of negativity and forget about it.

There are certain people who are ignorant of the way the world works. This ignorance can mean a person lives in fear, and this can make them react to the world in an angry way, by doing selfish things against other people, this can also happen when someone has died.

When there is a sudden death, the spirit is sometimes grounded, usually because the spirit has not realised it has died and therefore has not moved into the light or the spirit world. Sometimes the spirit refuses to move, especially if it feels that it has been a bad person on the earth plane and is scared of judgement on the other side (a belief from religious teachings). This would not actually be the case, as in the spirit realm the only judge is yourself; there is a clarity in the spirit world that does not exist here. These spirits can affect people. If someone was an alcoholic in life, their spirit may attach themselves to a bar in death.

Very rarely have I met someone who I think is a really bad person. Usually people who appear bad have an aura of negative energy brought about by their own fear.

Sometimes when you meet a person, you can see that they have a 'friend' with them; in other words, they are possessed. I have only met one person I thought was possessed, but the real him wasn't nice, even without the spirit possession, so I decided to leave well alone. There are spirit release (new name for exorcism) experts and it's always a good idea to have the number of one of these people on you, or to get trained to do it yourself.

If you do private readings, you may also come across some people with mental illness. A particular example I can remember was when a woman came into my office for a late-night appointment and promptly moved the chair in front of the door so that I wouldn't be able to get out of the room. She then became angry and began to be very rude, demanding to know her future. I talked her down, but it took half an hour. I had to explain that it was impossible to work with her if she held me captive in the room! I then discovered that she was waiting for me outside the front door of the building. Luckily, I was meeting a friend at my office, and an hour later I was safely escorted out of the building.

Another strange incident was when a man asked me to remove his underwear to do psychometry on his pants! Even though he was a gay man, he was sending sexual energy throughout the reading, something I dealt with in a very professional way after the tape had stopped.

These are just a few reasons why you should think twice about using your home as your office, as you don't always have time to vet people over the phone when booking appointments. Having said this, I must point out that it is easy to invite and create troublesome entities by worrying about them. It is good to know what is out there, but you should not dwell on it. For whatever reason, some people like to have dramas in their lives as it gives them an excuse for not living their time on this physical level of existence to its full potential. Whenever they run out of life drama scenarios (there is always a spiritual answer for those situations), they tend to take on the spirit drama of psychic attack and entities. Know yourself as an aspect of God and it just won't become part of your life experience or reality.

Thought forms – An entity that exists on the lower astral plane, brought into being by negative thinking. As all thoughts are creative, you can create your own negative pattern which, because like attracts like, will gain in energy.

Psychic vampires – People that draw energy from others to feed their own energy. This is not normally done deliberately, but better to have the intention to keep your own energy.

Psychic sponge – A person who picks up the feelings of others and takes them on as their own. Making sure you close your chakras, and having the intention of not picking up another's energy, can control this.

Geopathic stress – Created by electro-magnetic radiation, ley lines and underground streams. You can use dowsing as a way of finding out if this is a problem for you. The best way to combat this is to ask spirit to step in and fix it.

Intention – the best form of protection

There are many ways to clear negative energy out of a space and many ways to protect yourself from psychic attack, picking up others' negativity and losing your own energy to other people. The best way to begin is by listening to your intention towards others and yourself. The mind can be trained to use positive over negative; intention is the key. We are likely to be more protected and give out less negativity if we are grounded. Practicing the grounding meditation or doing any of the naturally grounding activities, perhaps as a treat to yourself, will help you remain balanced in your life. Prevention is better than cure; if we use psychic protection and grounding then we ourselves become less likely to damage other people by thoughtlessly sending out negative thoughts or feelings. The independent mind is strong, which means we can use it for the greater good of all through intention and responsibility.

Case study: Spiritual emergency

I once had to visit a woman who had problems dealing with the world. In fact, life had become so difficult for her that she couldn't leave the house. This is sometimes called a spiritual or psychic emergency, and happens when you do a lot of high vibrational work, such as meditation, but don't ground yourself or are not centred. One of her main problems was that she couldn't let people wear shoes in the house because she felt the negative energy picked up from the pavement; she also spent most of the day crying about the state of the world.

As I looked at her energy, I found that her aura was mostly out of her body and up to the left. However, she didn't want to ground herself as she preferred the detached, out-of-body feeling more than being connected to the earth. As a result, she had stopped eating. I explained to her that we are spirit beings having a physical experience and that whilst she was here she was meant to have an in-body experience.

Her reply was that she wanted to achieve enlightenment. There is nothing enlightening about starving to death and, once she became aware that it was the sensation of being out of the body that made her feel bad, she finally asked me what she could do to ground.

I said she needed to do some normal 'in-the-body' life things. She insisted that I tell how to be grounded in a spiritual way – should she close or open the chakras, was there a mantra? I eventually left her with the choices of singing and cleaning to concentrate on, two good ways of coming back to earth.

PART TWO

TUNING INTO SPIRIT

To successfully tune in to a higher level of vibration tuning, it really is important that the first level is working well. You must set down the foundations first, otherwise your energy vibrations may not be strong enough to make the next leap; it will be a bit like trying to make a call on a mobile phone with a weak signal!

Once you have discovered how your body feels when the chakras are open, practise how to heighten your energy awareness and receptivity, making sure that you are always able to ground yourself. Grounding your energy keeps you connected to the earth, which is especially helpful when working on a basic psychic level. When you feel confident that the foundations are established, you can move on to the next stage.

To reach higher levels of the astral plane for spirit communication, and to be as highly tuned as possible, the key is to be centred rather than grounded.

Tune vibration and being centred

The bottom three chakras – the root, sacral, and solar plexus – are the chakras linked to emotions within the ego. (The ego, despite its bad reputation, plays an important role whilst you are in the physical body, but it is important to make sure that it doesn't control your life.) Working with the bottom three chakras closed, we give more energy and intention to the other chakras – the heart, throat, third eye and crown. All of these are useful for connection to the spirit world, including our spirit guides and our higher self. Opening these chakras, while the lower ones are closed, will give you greater access to higher vibrational frequencies and dimensions.

When the higher chakras are open, it is important to be centred, otherwise you might become off-centred, which could make you feel a bit nauseous or prevent you from having complete control of the energy you are receiving, using or channelling out. This could result in not having enough awareness in the physical to operate effectively. To centre yourself you need to feel that you are totally balanced in mind and body.

Exercise: Tuning vibration and getting centred

Focus your attention on your breathing. As you take a few deep breaths, see the energy that you are breathing out journey up to each chakra in turn. With your intention, see the root chakra close, followed by the sacral chakra, then the solar plexus chakra.

Then breathe in, taking the energy of the in-breath and your intention down to the heart chakra and see the heart chakra open. Breathe in again, directing energy to the throat chakra and see it open. Continue to breathe in the energy in this way to open the third eye and then the crown chakra. Now visualise a long pole running through the centre of your body. You are held by this pole in a place of centredness.

Balancing your core male and female energies

Achieving a state of constant balance is important for everyday life, but especially for psychic work. When you are open to other energies, you are able to read a person. If you are not balanced and you read that a person doesn't like you or has a problem with you, it is likely that you will take it personally.

It is easy to say that you need to have dealt with all of your issues before you can help other people, but life is full of upcoming issues all the time. In my own experience, I have had to break up a relationship directly before an appointment with a client. As it turned out, my situation allowed me to feel great empathy for the client who was in the same situation. This shows exactly how spirit works, by bringing people together at just the right moment in their lives. That's something we can trust in.

Being able to be in balance is to be able to wobble, but not fall down. We need to allow space in our lives, even just two minutes of silence, for the opposing core energies (male and female) within us to harmonise. This also can be done through meditation, or through breathing in and visualising the core energy needed to create a balance. Take a look at the words below and see which fit into your everyday life.

Doing, Effort, Passive, Free, Still, Action, Thinking, Feeling, Intellect, Sensitive, Emotion and Rational.

Now see where they lie in the masculine and feminine core energy we have in all of us:

Masculine:	**Feminine:**
Doing	Being
Effort	Free
Action	Still
Thinking	Feeling
Intellect	Emotion
Rational	Sensitive

Masculine energy governs the left brain and the right-hand side of the body.

Feminine energy governs the right brain and the left-hand side of the body.

Often medical problems affecting one side of the body can be brought about by an imbalance in the male and female energy. Also, as a guide in a reading, if there is a scar or a mole or any other skin marking, this can be seen as an indication of problems or issues relating to the mother or the father, depending on whether the mark is on the right- or left-hand side of the face. Left female, right male.

Dealing with emotions

Emotions, whether your own or other people's, can also pull you off your point of centre. In everyday life we can be the victim of someone else's emotions and needs, none more so than those of us who decided to be born to serve other people and empower them. As people will be drawn to you when they are in an emotional state, it is good practice as a psychic to tune into their emotions in order to find out what they are. You can then work out how these emotions can positively serve a person, even if they feel bad as an experience.

We use emotions to identify and describe how we are feeling at any given moment. When we detect and identify the feeling it has become an emotion, an identified feeling. What has happened energy-wise is that the perception of an outside event has caused a response in the emotional body and, when this response is powerful enough, it will be experienced as a physical sensation in the physical body. The body then produces chemical signals that correspond to the emotion, and these chemical signals carry the emotional energy into every cell in the body. Our feelings will be determined not so much by what happens to us, but rather by the way we *perceive* what happens to us; in other words, by what our thoughts tell us about our situation. For example, when we do not get the job that we had hoped for we can tell ourselves that it was simply not meant to be and look forward to the next opportunity. Or we can bemoan our ill fortune, cursing the universe for denying us our big chance.

The body itself will also affect our mood. Emotions are experienced in the body; fear may manifest as a sick feeling in the pit of the stomach, whilst sadness may be felt around the heart centre. Sometimes we can change how we are feeling simply by adjusting our breathing and our posture.

Emotions are messages that provide a communication between our body and our spirit, with our mind as the mediator. Emotions may arise directly from the body, from past experiences, from our beliefs, from deep within the subconscious or from our higher self. An emotion is also a valuable tool in that it alerts you to a possible problem that needs your attention, but also brings with it the necessary energy to take action and tackle the problem.

When we experience an emotion, we tend to do one of three things. One reaction is to *express* the emotion – to put it out there. We may feel that we are being *made* to feel a certain way by someone else, in which case we may have some kind of emotional outburst, dumping all that energy outside of ourselves, often in the form of blame, self pity, anger or recrimination. We may feel justified in our response and possibly even feel better afterwards, but we are sentencing ourselves to repeat in the future the exact same patterns of behaviour that have led us to this point. Not to mention that releasing big negative farts of emotional energy into the space you share with others is just as anti-social and unpleasant as a real fart in a car.

Another option when we are experiencing a difficult emotion is to *repress* it, to ignore it and bottle it up, refusing to let it have any expression. This can lead to huge amounts of energy (usually negative) being actually stored in the body. The body is not designed as a storehouse for negativity, and eventually will register its *dis-ease* by making the person ill.

The third reaction is to try to honour and understand the emotion. This is the one to teach others to practise, if you can. Once we understand that our feelings and emotions can be a message from our authentic self, then we can accept the message and understand why we are feeling a particular way. As soon as that understanding enters into our reality, then immediately a catharsis or release takes place, allowing us to be subtly changed by the emotion. This, I believe, is partly why people sometimes have problems dealing with emotions – tackling an emotion involves change, and we resist change, many even fear it.

Another reason why we don't like to own and acknowledge emotions which we think of as negative, such as anger, jealousy or resentfulness, is that to do so labels us an angry/jealous/resentful person. Society gives us this unhelpful myth that good people do not experience bad feelings, meaning we do not deal with them. In fact, a situation that begins with emotional turmoil may lead you to a completely different experience of yourself, enabling you to achieve far grander dreams. Good and bad, right and wrong; these are relative judgements, not absolutes. Knowing this to be true will help you draw back to balance when your emotions make you feel out of control.

Case study: Emotional meeting

Sometimes in this line of work you may meet a client who has a genuine mental health problem. One client had fallen out with her family a number of years ago and, claiming that they were psychically attacking her, wanted me to protect her from them. Looking into this I could see that the woman was very unbalanced, with a split personality. In order to not move on in her life she had created a belief that her family was the root cause of all of her problems. No amount of explaining any of this was going to get through to her, and after a while she start attacking my work. In her mind, because I didn't agree with her, I must be wrong and she wouldn't even entertain the idea that I could be right. I tried to end the session without charging her, but she responded by saying that I didn't care about her and didn't want to help her.

Her imbalance became unmanageable for me, as nothing I said was going to make any difference. I had sensed from the moment she walked into my office that this might be the case, but I had decided to try and go ahead with the reading anyway. This was a good lesson for me, one that I now give you. In life, some people become so out of alignment with themselves that medical help is truly the only thing that will work for them, so don't lose your own alignment trying to rebalance another, as you may both fall overboard!

The balance of our emotions

All emotions can be placed somewhere on a spectrum that has **Love** at one end and **Fear** at the other. You might think that the opposite of love is hate, but love and hate are both horns on the same goat; they are born out of the same impulse. Hate is not the opposite of love. Hate is love corrupted by fear. Likewise, courage is not the opposite of fear, but rather love in spite of fear. In fact, love and fear are the only two emotions there are. Every other emotion is born of these two opposites. Thoughts and feelings at the love end of the spectrum are of a high, light, positive vibration; those at the fear end are of a lower vibration and will be dull, heavy, dense, and negative. Love is joyful, hopeful, trusting, and optimistic. Love brings you closer to the full experience of yourself and of life. Love joins us together, allowing us to see that we are all intimately connected. Fear is mistrustful. Fear tells you lies, tells you that there are things that you need that you do not have and you are in competition to get them. Fear separates us, isolates us. Fear justifies inflicting pain and suffering on others.

Fear is an emotion, but it cannot exist with out the ego. The two are very closely linked. Like the devil on one shoulder and an angel on the other shoulder.

Many of us think the fear voice can't be ego, as the ego thinks itself to be brilliant and above others. It is a form of self protection we wouldn't need, if we were fearless.

Ego attachment	**Spiritual attitude**
Fear	Love
Superiority	Equality
Competition	Cooperation
Problems	Challenges
Pessimism	Optimism
Control	Empowerment
Impatience	Patience
Jealousy	Detachment
Worry	Faith

Spirit guides

Although many people have different ideas about spirit guides, the fact remains that we are spirit having a physical experience and that guides are just spirit. At some stage, a spirit guide would have been a human being just like us and experienced a physical lifetime, but once it has left the physical world, it becomes pure spirit, in the same way we do. In short one day you might also be a spirit guide. To have a strong connection with spirit guides we need to become more like them (pure spirit), as they cannot manifest themselves physically. As we are both physical and spirit in being, the only way to achieve this is to raise our vibration.

Most people when they say they want a connection with their guides wait around for the guides to make a connection and give them a message, whereas in actual fact we, as the seeker of the message, should ask the questions. We should seek from spirit a cosmic answer to our life, and ask questions such as 'what am I meant to be doing?'

Our thoughts and wishes give spirit the task of bringing about what will best help us reach our spiritual goals in this lifetime. Not our financial goals, but our spirit ones. Who best to guide us than one who is already spirit, therefore without ego?

We can't lose the aspects of the physical world within our personality as they are needed to drive us forward in our life and our search. This is how we evolve, for without fear and the ego we wouldn't be able to protect the physical body, something that is vital to our experience of this dimension. The trick is to keep your personality in balance with your spirit self, so that when you reach the point you want to make a connection with your guide, you won't have as far to travel in vibration.

Who are spirit guides?

I can only talk from my own personal experience of my spirit guides; our own individual experiences are quite unlike anyone else's, much in the same way that I wouldn't expect you to have the exact same friends as me. Spirit guides are as personal as our friendships. In fact, they are our greatest friends.

I have never been judged by my guides, or told I am wrong, or told what to do. Many of us believe our guides want us to work for them, thinking 'I have to work for spirit as a medium', 'I am the chosen one!' But spirit would support you whatever your way of life.

Your first contact with a spirit guide was before you were born. Before you entered this world, you had a chat with spirit about what you wanted to experience in this lifetime, what you wanted to learn and feel. I like to imagine that you were given a pre-birth questionnaire, offering a selection of tick boxes! You were then assigned a guide whose job is to help you follow the right path. The lessons are then relayed to you through your feelings.

A guide can come from a past life and, on rare occasions a member of your family may become a guide, although this happens only when they are relatively evolved. My mother is wonderful, but I have hardly listened to her in this lifetime, and it is likely that she won't attain the spirit guide level until after a few more lifetimes, as I'm sure I won't either.

From my experience Spirit doesn't manifest itself to you in a physical sense or use a name, but instead communicates through telepathy. It's as if you know someone is talking to you but you cannot see them. Likewise, if I send an intention in the form of a thought to a person, they receive it without consciously being aware that I am sending it. People often have an urge to know where the spirit guide is from, but spirit is beyond identity, and this is something that the great British medium Gordon Smith was hinting at when he said, 'The American Indian spirit guides are for the cowboy mediums.' In a sense Smith is right, but let's not forget that American Indians were the first documented mediums who practiced rituals in order to communicate with their ancestors. So, who could be better than the American Indians as guides for mediums today?

The desire to know where a spirit guide comes from originates from our ego and our need for physical connection, and it can be generally said that we all feel more confident about our mediumship if we have an amazing spirit guide. One of my guides, who I named Marcus due to not understanding his full name (as he said, 'it's **so** unimportant!), told me he was a bricklayer from Essex. I was **so** disappointed, but it was a lesson as it's not where the guide has been in a past life that is important, rather it's who they are to you in this life. Marcus was right, a name is irrelevant.

Many guides will talk to you through the mind using the same voice as you hear in your thoughts. After all, guides don't have a voice box! But if you concentrate, you will find the speech pattern is actually different in rhythm and vibration from your normal thoughts.

Sometimes, you may have 'downloads' of knowledge, not quite realising the moment the information came, but suddenly somehow just knowing. This is quite an effective way of receiving help from spirit.

When you are doing a reading, you may also see lights around people which lets us know spirit is around; this could even be the person's spirit guide. During a reading, if a person wants to have a connection with their guide you can ask the guide to touch your client's hair or skin. Personally, when I need physical contact from my guide I simply put my hand on my right shoulder and my guide puts his hand on mine. In truth, spirits are beads of light. They know it is important for us to occasionally have a physical sign from them, but, for proper communication, it is essential that we move up to their level of vibration. We must not attempt to bring spirits down to our own physical level.

Our collective guide group change all the time. As our vibration levels rise, so our spirit guides change to keep in tune with our heightened vibrations. It seems that we work with guides who are a few vibrations above our own, which means the higher you tune your vibration, the brighter the light-being you will be working with, right up into the angelic realm.

There are many psychics who claim to work with angels. It is true that angels help humans, but remember that they have never been in a physical body and therefore have less connection with us here than spirit guides have. I ask angels for help on large world issues rather than personal ones, mainly because my spirit guides work perfectly well for me on an everyday basis. Angels will always try and help in the way that you asked, whereas guides will know that you have to go through whatever suffering you feel you are going through for your own greater good.

One of my students once asked me if Angels ever lie. I said 'no' as they have no ego and therefore no need to lie. I inquired as to why she had asked the question. She replied, 'Well, I asked my angels if I should get analogue or broadband internet, and they clearly said analogue, so I got analogue, but now I find that broadband would have been better!' I did point out that angels don't use the internet. This might sound like this person is daft, but it's amazing how the wave of interest in angels has opened up all sorts of misunderstanding of the spirit world.

Muddling through life, getting things wrong, sorting them out and moving on **is** the meaning of life. Running to find your spirit guide every time something goes wrong isn't appropriate to the role of the guide. If and when you are really stuck, turn to spirit for help and, like a teacher, your guide will give you a different way to look at solving the problem but never the answer.

I think the best psychic mediums work in the same way as spirit, needing to be a few vibrational levels above the clients, which is why your clients change as you change in vibrational frequency. If you have a low vibrational client then they won't understand what you are saying. The best help you can give a person is a different perspective so that they can figure it out for themselves. This works along the same principle as building a well rather than handing out a glass of water.

It's good to remember that not all spirit guides know everything and you may even, at some point, be a medium for a spirit going through their guideship.

I have met a few advanced mediums who have been visited by a novice spirit accompanied by a guide who uses the medium's experience to help train the novice spirit into becoming a guide for a new medium. Everyone has to start somewhere!

Many of you will already have a connection with the one spirit guide that stays with you for life, better known as your 'gatekeeper', or 'doorkeeper'. In my life this is Marcus. This guide 'vets' which guides will work with you to make sure you don't become vibrationally fried by the wrong guide frequency. Your gatekeeper can also be the vibration translator for your mediumship, although many mediums work directly with the dead person the client is trying to contact. In my mediumship, my guide brings forward the information from the spirit. We work like this because I can understand and communicate with my guide clearly, but it's also because I haven't 'sat in the power' for long enough. Whilst mediums take years to develop to a level of excellence, I myself am too impatient and, as I feel that being a medium is only a small part of my work, I haven't taken the time to develop fully.

One of the reasons that, in the last few years, I have seen mediums develop at an amazing rate is due to the change in the vibration on the planet; this has caused many more children to be born psychic and mediumistic. One day no one feel the sense of grief and loss that death brings, if we can visit our loved ones every night in our dreams.

My mediumship does allow me to channel lots of wisdom from some amazing beings, but sometimes in a reading I might just forward a simple message instead of giving long, detailed information, as many other mediums might do in a sitting. This is because when I tune into the spirit of a dead person, I do it via my guide and he is able to advise me first on the best way to relay the information to my client. Say, for example, another medium was talking directly to the spirit of a woman's father, she would then go ahead and describe the father's personality and appearance, give a message and end the reading with a spiritualist saying which many mediums use: 'That's just his way of showing you he's around you'. If it then turned out this man used to sexually abuse his daughter, this message would not have the same loving effect as it would on a woman who simply missed her father and had not been abused by him. In this instance, if I was the medium, my gatekeeper would have informed me that the information was delicate and warned me to be careful on how I presented the message.

I have had the spirit of the husband of a woman come through and tell his wife 'not long now love,' referring to how long she still had to live. She was overjoyed with the news as she had cancer and couldn't wait to join him, and I would have felt difficult about giving that message if it hadn't been vetted by Marcus first.

Due to us having free will, spirit can't help us unless we ask. When I was thinking about changing my whole way of life and working with spirit, I gave a list of things I felt I needed, the first request being to own my own home. As I worked as a self-employed stage manager, getting a mortgage was near impossible. Working as a psychic medium and starting a career from the bottom was going to mean I wouldn't be able to buy a house for a long, long time, so I asked spirit to find a way to make it possible. It took a few months, but one day a friend of mine called Dave told me he wanted to invest in property, without having the hassle of lodgers. Did I want to buy a house with him? So he provided the deposit and I got a mortgage. After three years, I re-mortgaged on the profit from the property and bought Dave out. I got my house!

The second thing I asked for was an understanding boyfriend. After all, being a psychic is not something many people would really appreciate, and it would make me less compatible, especially as I've always been a bit of an odd shape to be compatible with. The next relationship I had was with a man whose mother was a psychic and father was a healer. We were together for four years and it was in that time that my education bloomed. If you are looking to make a way of life for yourself from doing the work of your higher self, for the purpose of good and the well-being of others, then spirit will move mountains, but you have to you ask.

As our guides change so much, it is important to keep sitting with them in meditation every day, if you can, just to feel who is around you. It is not always possible to do this but it is worth the effort as once a strong connection is made it's like riding a bike; you will never forget how to do it, but need practice to avoid wobbling. I have been, on occasion, stopped in the street by my guides who have told me to stop walking and sit down whilst they talk to me. Normally it has been to prompt a most profound realisation of my own foolish behaviour in that moment, a kind of 'you do realise that…' moment. If you take the time to connect with your guide, then you can have this kind of contact at any time, whilst constantly building a stronger connection. But be aware of your own vibration changing, as well as your work changing, before it comes as a surprise.

As I work through my guides for mediumship, there are some points in my life when they turn the mediumship off. This could be because I've got my own emotional life going on and this level of work might be a little too much, or it may simply be that I'm not resting enough or that I'm going through a major vibrational shift. It's good to know where you are at, so you can keep clients in the picture and, if necessary, recommend them on to somebody else. Recommendation doesn't mean that you think someone is a better medium than you, it simply means that it may just be what's needed at that time, especially as the client's needs should always come first.

If you're not great with meditation or if you are very busy, then there are many ways to contact your guide. These include: automatic writing, psychic art, asking questions and looking for patterns or coincidences.

Exercise: Meditation to meet your spirit guide

It may be helpful to make a tape of the instructions to play back in order to allow you to follow the meditation without referring to this book.

Take a moment to focus your attention on your breathing.

Open up your chakra centres as discussed in Part One. Know that you are connected to the spirit world, which is not above you but all around you.

Visualise before you a flight of stairs going up. There are five steps with a door at the top.

Your body feels at ease as you take the first step.

With the second step you feel more relaxed.

With the third step your body is stress-free and your mind is calm.

With the fourth step you feel lighter.

With the final step you open the door.

It takes a moment for your eyes to adjust to the light, but not far in front of you is a building made of crystal and glass. You have seen this place before and it makes you feel at home. Make your way towards it, noticing its beauty as you go.

Upon your arrival the door opens, welcoming you. Inside, the sunlight casts rainbows all around the room, through the crystal walls.

Take a moment to absorb this breathtaking sight.

There is a bench and you take a moment to sit in this energy with your eyes closed.

As you sit you feel someone is joining you.

You know this is your spirit guide. There is no need to open your eyes.

Greet your guide.

Your spirit guide has something to say to you. You may hear this now.

If you have any questions for your guide, ask them now.

Thank your guide for the information given. You may even be given a hug before they leave you.

It is time to come back now.

So take your leave of the castle, knowing that this is your safe space and you can return back here any time you want to.

The door is open and you are ready to climb back down the stairs.

With your first step, you are reminded of your own personal strength.

With your second step, you are reminded of all the love you have had in your life.

With the third step you remember all the beauty in the world.

With the fourth step your body feels young, healthy and full of life.

With the last step, you feel grateful for all your blessings.

Turn the lights off at each of your chakra points.

Make sure you are grounded and protected.

When you are ready, bring yourself back into the room and open your eyes.

Communication with spirit

You are spirit having a physical experience, whereas spirit is non-physical. Remember, it is so much easier for your spirit to make connection with pure spirit, rather than expecting non-physical spirit to become physical without birth!

No doubt many of you have read books were the author tells the story of how their guide or angel became physical in the room with a message for them, but I am sure that this is not as common as the stories themselves! I know of a famous author and expert in angels who completely over-exaggerated the angelic encounter they had in order to sell the story. The only thing wrong with that for me is that it makes others feel they don't have a great connection with their guides, causing them to discount all of the small ways spirit try to communicate with us every day.

Guardian angels may never have been in physical form. Often I find spirit guides have greater empathy because they have been physical and remember the restrictions of the body and the ego.

Automatic writing

This is a wonderful way to connect to your guides. It is not strictly speaking 'automatic': you have to start the writing, using words from your own mind, then spirit takes over from you. Usually, by the time you have finished writing, the channel will have started.

Before you start, make a mental decision that you only want to hear your own spirit guides, otherwise it's like opening the front door and inviting anyone in off the street. We only invite to a communication the quality speakers! Often it is good to start with a word in mind, for example, 'strength'. Then simply start writing around that word, and allow what follows. The trick to this is not to consciously try at all, but just allow your hand to write the words that come to you and see where it leads you. If you are expecting your hand to become possessed and start writing without any command from you, you may be waiting a long time! You will still have to actually write down the words as they come to you, but they are coming from beyond you. It is like a train of thought that rises by itself and you are taking dictation from it. This is the right way to do automatic writing. Simply leaving your hand with a pen on a page and drawing letters to see what few words spirit has to say isn't the quality of work we are looking for.

This kind of communication can also be done with voice and a tape recorder in which case it would become inspirational speaking.

The good old-fashioned ways

Sometimes the old way of doing things, such as in the Victorian era when spiritualism was at its heyday, can still be used today.

It was during the Victorian era that the séance, as we know it today, evolved. The Fox sisters, at the forefront of the first spiritualist movement in America, claimed that they discovered the phenomenon of spirit rapping, that spirit communicated by making tapping noises – 'Once for yes, twice for no'. Originally it was seen as a weird form of entertainment, but things changed as it became apparent something more was happening and much of the information received from spirit was correct. Slowly, the movement began to spread throughout the world. Séances were normally held in a darkened parlour, with a group of guests and the medium sitting around a table. Over the years, the spiritualist movement found that it could help the connection by using props or tools, such as a small bell hung from a frame so that spirit could shake it, or an ear trumpet placed on the table, in case the spirit wanted to speak. As a result, the phenomena began to be known as physical mediumship. Table tipping was then introduced and thereafter theatrics became more and more common as pranksters faked the process.

There are many stories of people becoming possessed by evil spirits when trying to make spirit communication. Make sure that the people you are working with have the intention of light and love in their wish to communicate, otherwise, when you start trying to contact ghosts or other members of the spirit world, you may be opening a different type of door. I don't make random phone calls to talk to just anyone, or leave my front door open with the word 'party' written on it…

Table tipping

Table tipping was extremely popular as a Victorian parlour game. However, it is now a highly-rated form of spirit communication, although many still do not take it seriously. The energy that builds during a session is that of joy.

A group of people sit or stand around a circular wooden table with their palms down, fingertips on the table's surface. The medium protects the group with white light, or in any way they see fit, and then verbally asks spirit guide to come to the table and communicate with them. When the spirit guide arrives, all the sitters feel a warming energy fill the circle of people, often with a build up of that energy over their hands, as if the spirit was putting its hands on top of theirs. The table may vibrate and the medium will then ask the spirit to tip the table. It is then possible for the spirit to answer questions, in the form of two tips for ‘yes’ and one tip for ‘no’.

Glass divination

Not to be confused with the Ouija board which, in my experience, comes up with information that isn’t accurate, and, in addition, its bad press only conjures up old fears. Glass divination is used in the same way as table tipping, whereby people position themselves in a circle around a table and place their fingertips on a glass that is situated up-turned in the middle of a table. The glass will then move as the energy builds, sometimes quite violently, in circles around the table. Similar to table tipping, the spirit can ask the glass to move for ‘yes’, and stop for ‘no’. It is not the best way to communicate with spirit guides, but still a method of doing it. Make sure that you set out your intention by making it clear you want to communicate with your guides.

Psychic art

Some psychics allow their hands to be used by spirits for painting, drawing or, in some cases, sculpturing. The psychic artist can draw spirit guides, past loved ones or even angels. To be a good artist you need to have the technical art skills to start with, although some artists say they have been taught how to draw by their guides.

Exercise: Drawing your guide

Allow yourself some quiet time. Whether you are using a whole paint pad, pastels, crayons or a biro pen, psychic art should always come from the same space you are in when you are doodling. Don’t try for the image, simply allow the image to come and you might find the results are very satisfying. It is important to remember that this is a drawing of your guide in one lifetime. Your guide might be choosing a life that will resonate with you the most. In spirit form, guides are round beads of light and don’t take human form as they are not in the human body.

Mediumistic communication and proof of life

It is unfortunate that, as with many other industries, people don't understand the terms we use. Often a person will book for a reading when they mean a sitting. Every medium has passed the psychic vibration, meaning that every medium is psychic, but not every psychic is a medium. So if a person would like to have contact with someone in the spirit world, they would go for a sitting to see a medium.

It is a wonderful gift to be able to offer people, the gift of contact and peace of mind. What any medium is looking to do at the start of a sitting is give information to the client from the communicator (i.e. the spirit of the dead person) about who they were in life and what they were like. This will provide proof that the right spirit is coming through with a message.

Description of the communicator:	Clothes, sex, age, height, nationality, hair, distinguishing marks: scars, tattoos, etc.
Presentation of communicator:	Smart, neat and tidy, uniform, scruffy, biker, fashion-conscious, etc.
Relationship of the communicator to the sitter:	Parent, friend, lover, spouse, aunt, cousin, uncle, niece, in-laws, work colleague, etc.
Character of the communicator:	Moody, happy, free-spirit, shy, out-going,

	laid-back, compulsive, grumpy, etc.
Mental state of the communicator:	Sharp, intelligent, deep, slow, depressed, etc.
Emotional state of the communicator:	Sensitive, loving, up-beat, disowned, upset, etc.
Mannerisms of the communicator:	Nervous disorders, stroking chin, rubbing hands, pushing glasses, biting nails, unusual walk, twirling rings, etc.
Unusual habits of the communicator:	Always checking the gas is off, always called on a Friday, always wore a hat, etc.

Communication is a three-way conversation

The medium communicates with the spirit (communicator), then the medium talks to the sitter. As a medium, listen clearly but be aware that you must communicate with the spirit, ask information and let the spirit know and feel that you will try your best to give clear, factual information. The sitter may still be suffering grief so try to be as clear and sensitive as you can and allow a little time for them to think about what you are saying, because you are dealing with strong emotions, such as love, regret, sorrow, humour and anger from both worlds.

Platform mediumship

What is the point of a mediumship demonstration? A spirit needs the energy of the living to be able to work well in this physical dimension, and a room full of people, especially when giving a demonstration on a platform or a stage, provides good conditions for communication, as there is much more energy for the spirit to work with. Mediumship demonstrations are the strongest way to give evidence of continued life after death, as the audience witnesses a clear communication with a spirit that has the same mind and personality as it had in life (with a bit more wisdom). The audience also sees that this spirit is aware of what is going on in the life of the person they wish to communicate with. The only drawback of a big demonstration is that the medium and client may suffer from distractions in a room full of people and as a result it may be more difficult to pass on the message.

Why spirit comes through

Each spirit will have a different reason for the communication; it is important to ask the spirit why they have come through and make sure the person in the audience knows they are hearing the opinion of the spirit. The spirit cannot make decisions for us; we have free will, so avoid answering questions such as ‘Does Dad want me to marry Freddy?’

Making a link

After giving a full description of the communicating spirit, if you are not drawn to one particular person or no one has come forward to claim the spirit, stop and ask if anyone recognises the description. Don’t do this too soon; make sure you have given detail.

Once you have the communicator placed, give more information about personality and mannerisms. If still no one can take the person after all the information you have, ask the spirit to draw back and ask for someone else to take their place. Rather than see this as a failure, think in your mind that the audience member will realise the link that the spirit was for them at another time and feel comforted they got some information.

It is important to get a clear response from the audience member as their voice can help you build your link with the energy from spirit. At the same time, a loud response allows the audience to know that the person receiving the message has identified the spirit.

If names and information cannot be placed, go back to the energy of the spirit and ask for more information. If most of the information has been accepted, it is then probable the recipient will be able to confirm the unplaced information later. This can provide the best evidence, as it proves you are not picking up information psychically from the receiving person. However, refrain from leaving the recipient with too much unrecognised information, otherwise it will look like wrong information, covered up as information the recipient doesn't happen to know; this won't look good to an audience.

Preparation for a demonstration

Atmosphere –	Small hall or theatre, private room or church, all Suitable.
Audience –	Be prepared for a mixture of believers, sceptics, antagonistics, people too scared to talk in a room full of people and the plain curious.
Medium –	Ensure that health, mental state, emotional state, spiritual place are well tuned.
Spirit –	Look for experience in communication, emotional state, intellectual state, personality.

True spirit evidence occurs on an emotional level, when we touch the soul of another with the energy of unconditional love of God and the spirit world.

Delivering a message

Part 1 – Beginning the message. The spirit has made an initial link with you; this will be felt in the aura as the spirit draws close. The information the spirit brings to your consciousness may not be very clear as the link is building, but as you pass on each bit of information to the sitter, the spirit will feel more comfortable with you and will then draw closer. This in turn allows information to become clearer.

Part 2 – At this stage, a member of the audience begins to identify the spirit and this is when the communication is at its strongest; this is the time for you find out the reason why the spirit came forward, i.e. the message. The vibration is at its strongest at this point, and you can really take advantage of it. The more acknowledgement you can get from the audience member in terms of a positive recognition of information, the stronger the link will build.

Part 3 – Once the bulk of the information has been put across, the spirit will start to withdraw and the information will become less clear. This is a good point to stop as you could undo all of the good work you have just done by then saying the wrong thing. This would make everything you said previously look like a lucky guess.

Spirit release

The area of work you choose to specialise in will largely depend upon what people come to see you for. At some point you will find that a person comes to you with the belief that they, or a person in their life, has a spirit or entity attachment.

Sometimes, the spirit of a person can be left on this earth when someone dies because it has not changed vibration and therefore not moved on to the astral plain. In effect, the dead person's spirit has passed by the open doorway to the spirit world.

Spirit release is like opening the door in the vibration of the beleaguered spirit. To do this, we, as mediums, use our physical vibration and blend it with the vibration of spirit. Blending the two worlds together in this way enables the earthbound spirit to make the transformation with ease. The simplest way to carry out this release is to call the appropriate people together from this and the other side of life, and then, by having the intention of the greater good, we can ask our angels and guides to take the grounded spirit to a place that is best for them. Not everything belongs to the light.

If you are interested in the practice of spirit release, there are many great books on the subject. I can recommend one by Sue Allen, who incidentally was my teacher in this subject, called *Spirit Release,* published by O Books.

Physical mediumship

Physical mediumship is when a medium and a spirit try to give evidence of the existence of spirit through physical means, such as moving or apporting an object (by bringing an object not originally from the space into the space). Physical mediumship differs from mental mediumship in that it requires the phenomenon to be experienced by the physical five senses. This type of mediumship was popular in the Victorian times, but aspects of the practice, such as Ectoplasm, are rarely seen today.

The most common understanding of ectoplasm is that it is green and sticky. This image is the media's interpretation and in the film *Ghostbusters*, which coined the phrase 'I've been slimed', the poor intrepid ghostbusters were constantly being covered in a goo, ejected from a spook. This, of course, is far from the true meaning.

Ectoplasm (which comes from the Greek words *ektos* and *plasma*, meaning 'exteriorised substance') is in fact a white substance that comes from a medium's facial orifices, such as nostrils, eyes or ears. In the past, a séance was normally conducted in red light which made any white fabric look red, but, interestingly, the ectoplasm produced stayed white.

To produce ectoplasm, the medium went into a 'trance state' and allowed spirit to make the substance. Spirit then moulded the substance into the face of the person who had died, through which the spirit would often talk to its loved ones by passing on facts that only they knew. Sometimes the medium's assistant would attach the 'face' to an ear trumpet as an amplifier. Occasionally, the spirit would take on complete human form (still attached to the medium) and physically interact with their loved ones. At the end of the séance the ectoplasm would disappear back into the medium's body.

To this day, we still don't know what the full chemistry of ectoplasm is. Due to its likeness to cheesecloth, many of the Victorians felt the medium was regurgitating yards of cheesecloth from the stomach, ears or nostrils, which in itself would be an amazing feat!

I remember a story I once heard at Arthur Findley College when I was studying there. Gordon Higginson, a physical medium, was once found to have a pin inside his body. He hadn't swallowed it, nor was there any pinhole within his body. The pin must have been picked up by the ectoplasm (which has a sticky surface) when the substance was absorbed back into his body.

Helen Duncan

One of the best-known physical mediums, Helen Duncan was unfortunately tried for witchcraft under the Act 1735, even though her trial was in the 1950s.

During the time of the Second World War, Helen Duncan's séances were extremely popular as she produced the physical form of a dead person using ectoplasm. People whose loved ones had died were in desperate need to communicate one last time. Shockingly, it was during one séance that some mothers first heard of their loved ones being killed in action; their beloved sons and husbands appeared through ectoplasm to bring them the terrible news in person. It seemed that the government had not yet released the information to the next of kin.

This was the case for one mother when she attended a séance held by Mrs Duncan: she was shocked to see the ectoplasm that poured out of the medium turn into her son. He told her his ship had sunk and that he had died. Terrible news for anyone, but at least she saw him and said her goodbyes. Eventually, the mother decided to contact the Navy and ask them to confirm the sinking of HMS Barnum, as well as the fact that her son had perished. The Navy were stunned as this sinking was not public knowledge and the Navy's intelligence was actually, at that time, unaware of the sinking of the ship. When news of the ship's sinking eventually broke to the military intelligence, Helen Duncan was immediately seen as a threat to security and the military stormed into one of the séances. Despite the fact that Helen's spirit guide had given her warning of this event, she continued with the séance. If a medium who is producing ectoplasm is disturbed, the ectoplasm will return back into the body far too quickly, causing internal burning and bleeding. Helen consequently became ill, but her trial still went ahead and she was found guilty of witchcraft.

This type of communication seems primitive when you put it in the context of the technological age. Spirits, like us, have moved on and are taking advantage of all the electrical forms of communication. It is my belief that spirit will find ways to communicate using such things as computers or televisions. Already, there have been claims that spirit faces have been seen through television's white noise. I try to not encourage this practice because it needs to be done in a controlled environment, with a suitably experienced medium present. Think of it as opening your front door: what would happen if you left your front door open? Anyone could come in.

As the earth moves forward towards the spiritual age, psychics and mediums become mainstream. Many successful ghost-hunting TV programmes now include the séance as one of their experiments. The first ever séance to be shown on TV was back in the nineties and was watched by 30 million viewers worldwide. I myself performed a live séance over the radio for Halloween 2005. Of course, the reality of séances is still denied by a sceptical few. In 2004, Derren Brown the illusionist managed to hoax a séance live on TV to prove to the public they can be tricked. The show became one of the most complained-about TV programmes in television history.

Exercise: EVP – electronic voice phenomena

EVP is an alleged recording of voices of the dead which occurs at a higher frequency to our own. It is said that EVP can be picked up by tape and video recorders.

Place a recording device in a room. It helps if the room is thought to be active with spirit phenomenon – you will have better results from spirits if they can use energy from that dimension to communicate. However, it doesn't matter if there doesn't happen to be any activity in the room at that time. Say out load in the room that you wish to communicate with spirit, then let the spirit know your intentions to record its voice. Turn the recorder on and leave the room. Come back later and listen to the results. This can also be done with a group of people in a circle, would raise the energy for the EVP to take place.

Transfiguration

'Transfiguration' is when the spirit overlays its face upon the mediums and is seen best in red light or when filmed and played back through a TV. The medium's spirit still stays in the body, it is only the facial features that look as though they are changing into another person.

Trance mediumship

Trance is a blending of the spirit with the medium. Using the spoken word, the spirit can use the medium's body to communicate in this physical world.

Trance is seen to be the strongest degree of control that spirit has over the medium, yet there are various degrees of trance control: from light trance to very deep trance, depending upon the intent and conditions of the medium and spirit.

In the trance condition, the spirit communicator is speaking directly through the consciousness of the medium, rather than the medium relating what is being mentally given to him or her by the spirit. The voice pattern, inflection, and general manner of speech is different from the normal voice of the medium. It does not mean that the medium is, in any way, possessed by a spirit personality. Possession is extremely rare as the spirit of the medium stays in the medium's body at all times.

PART THREE

BEING AN ASPECT OF GOD

I see the psychic as being very much like a musical instrument in that he or she needs to be finely tuned. A psychic requires a high level of sensitivity in order to tune into the different vibrations of the world. There is a saying that the world is made of sound, and this, in truth, is very much the case. When we look into metaphysics, we can see that everything is made of vibrating matter, vibrating molecules. And if we could hear the reverberations of each level of vibration of this earth, the sound would be rather deafening. A psychic spends their life tuning into different frequencies of vibration, and many people are born with the ability to do this. In actual fact, as the frequencies of the earth are changing, we can see that within our children different frequencies are being born. There's much talk of indigo children and crystal children who are born with psychic ability and intense sensitivity, and how they are going to be the ones to change the world into a better place.

This book is very much for anyone who wants to live in a modern world where they can actually change their vibrational frequency. For a long time now we've treated changing frequency as a kind of party trick, enabling us to know some things that we couldn't possibly know. Highly-tuned psychics are able to pick up on people's past and their present, and give bits and pieces of information about the future. The most successful psychics today are the ones who have actually blended this ability with a holistic approach to life, and are now coaching, counselling and giving advice from a self-help perspective. Other psychics, the ones that I deem to be old-fashioned, are the ones who still believe in predicting the future which, in my mind, is like handing out a cup of water of hope where there is the potential to build someone an entire well.

Most of us live life along set patterns, going through the same things time and time again, thereby suppressing emotions and deadening our senses. Sometimes we actually question why we live this like, but more often we simply tell ourselves that this behaviour is just part of our personality. Modern psychotherapy, teaches us to look at the way we grew up and to actually go through the process of facing any hurt of the past and bringing it into our present. Of course, as we discover that the world is not the way we'd perceived it to be, we begin to learn that all of our thoughts are creative. The modern psychic's approach is to help us recognise that, with all thoughts being creative, it is good to understand where the patterns in our lives come from. Then, creatively, with our full expression of being, we can obliterate the patterns and start again, afresh, changing the decisions that we made in childhood in order to make a brand new start towards the future.

But, of course, this is where a psychic can really empower a client over a psychotherapist, or anyone else in other practical, helpful counselling roles, because we hopefully have the vision to be able to see, with great clarity, someone's past and therefore understand their present situation. What an advanced psychic can do is take this much, much further by tuning in a person's vibrational frequency to be able to communicate with the spirit world, thereby bringing forward messages from dead friends and relatives in the same way as a medium.

On a level beyond that, the psychic is able to be in touch with a person's spirit guides, gaining access to the soul's consciousness. A step on from that is the angelic realm which brings forward great healing and positive energy. If somebody needs a great and intense healing or clearing, then the angelic realm is one that the psychic can tune into, or rather, the psychic medium.

On the next level up, the psychic medium attunes him/herself to the highest frequency they can possibly attain within the physical body, enabling him/herself to have connection with the Akashic records. At this level of consciousness, a psychic is all-seeing and all-knowing and is actually able to bring forward information. Spirit guides are also found at this Akashic level and if you have good communication with your guides, they can give you the Akashic information. In effect, at this level you are working as a spirit guide whilst still in the physical body. This is only appropriate on occasion and must be carefully controlled by your own and the client's spirit guides.

In the Akashic records we have the knowledge, in a sense, of the whole world as it stands, but I have a feeling that this amount of knowledge should really be the privilege of the people who are not in the physical body. I've often spent much of my time asking spirit, 'What's it like in the spirit world?', 'What's it like when you die?', 'What's it like to miss your friends and relatives?', 'What does it feel like to fly?', 'What's it like to be the closest vibration of light?' The answers that come back to me are never really what I want. I'm never really told exactly what it's like to be in the spirit world, and my understanding is that I am probably unable to comprehend it.

So what we're looking for is to raise our vibrational frequency so that we have access to these records, and at the same time, our spirit guide will show us how much knowledge we can take on board without frying our brains. Bear in mind that in order to get to that height of vibrational frequency, you actually have to have gone through a myriad of life experiences, using the best quality of vibration you can manage. If you do not have this experience, this energy would be simply too much for you. If you can actually attain that aspect of your life and achieve that quality of vibrational frequency then it is true that absolutely anything will be possible with regards to access of information.

However, the information gained must be strictly for the client only, and limited to whatever it is deemed fit for the client to know at that particular time, such as information about somebody's past life. You wouldn't be able to see the entirety of that person's past life, but what you would get, perhaps, is a glimpse of why they are going through a particular current situation. An example of this would be if you were trying to help a woman who was very overweight and you saw that in a previous life the woman had been imprisoned in a concentration camp where she had been starved. This would explain why that person, in this lifetime, is particularly overweight – due to her previous deprivation, she feels that she needs to gorge herself when food is around and when it is actually possible to eat. So, by clearing and healing, or bringing to attention the past life situation, we can actually go some way towards being able to heal a person with a weight difficulty in this lifetime.

Also, within the Akashic records you'll be able to see the soul groups – the groups of people that you have chosen to reincarnate with. This could include a current partner, your father, your mother, siblings and friends. If you are working with a client, you will be able to see the client's soul group and be able to find out how they were linked in a previous life. You can forge a communication to deal with any issues that the client may have with the soul group. For example, if your client had promised someone in a previous lifetime that they would stay with them forever, that might be why in this lifetime they're having real difficulty in ending the relationship. You can probably understand the potential of gaining access to these records, and will recognise that this is a far cry from the psychic 'fortune telling' readings of the past. Work on this level is about clearing blocks from people's lives in order to help them reach their highest vibrational frequency.

In order to do this work, you need to clear your own blocks first. Many people in the helping profession desperately want to be helpers, healers and counsellors in order to feel good about themselves. My attitude is that you need to feel good about yourself and be able to prioritise yourself first before you're going to be able to reach this highest level of vibrational frequency, because if you spend your entire life helping, serving and dealing with other people, you won't give enough time to yourself and this can only build resentment. This kind of resentment will block you from moving up into the highest vibrational frequency of love. You will need to deal with all these issues before you move on, and later on, we will look at how to help you remove these blocks.

By removing our blocks of resistance we become more colourful and joyful people. As colour and sound resonate to different frequencies, very much like the colours of the chakra: red, orange, yellow, green, blue, indigo and white. Each of these colours corresponds with the sounds Do Re Me Fa So La Ti and Do, whereby Do is actually God which, in a sense, we look at ourselves as being – God representation in physical form, or light form.

Imagine that we started off being God. There was only God, one creative energy, and then a question that crossed God's mind, 'What if?' This created a split. We are now God experiencing itself. As we head toward 2012 we are heading back towards the homeward journey, recognising that we are not individuals but all one. There is no such thing as separation: we are, in fact, all joined in oneness and the closer we come to that realisation, the closer we come to realising that we have access to everybody's spiritual records – as long as we have the right frequency of vibration. By having access to these records we are learning how closely linked we all are; how related we are to one another. We are discovering that many of our lifetimes have been spent with each other several times over, with the person who saved your life in one lifetime possibly being the person that you try to beat to the seat on the bus in this lifetime.

There are so many inter-connections between us that we are, literally, God. We are God currently experiencing individuality, in the process of going back to the understanding that there is no separation between us, only oneness, otherwise understood as God. It is from this understanding about this feeling of oneness that we have the desire to help people. However, to form this understanding of oneness we must also recognise that there is no such thing as death, because if we are all one then surely we must also be a part of those who are already in the spirit world. Only through this realisation will we be able to have constant communication with our dead friends and relatives, even if we can't see them.

The heightening of our vibrational frequency (not just ours, but of the plants, the earth and the animals) is actually going to give us the gift of being mediums for ourselves; to have communication with our spirit guides, as well as with our dead friends and loved ones, and to help us understand each other, the animals, the plants and the earth so much better than we currently do. This is my hope for the future, for without this hope I really honestly believe that human life on earth is doomed. If we don't follow a more spiritual path (that feeling of oneness and unity) and practice a more holistic approach, there will only be bleakness ahead. At this rate, the earth is going to wipe us out long before we even get to a point where pollution or global warning actually finish us off, as I believe that the earth will just take back its own. On the other hand, I can't truly believe that we human beings are stupid enough to continue along this destructive path. We need to conquer our fear, however, for this is what stops us from seeing beyond our enclosed lives; we are living in a world that is crying out for healing, yet we seem unable to hear its cries.

Through this part of the book we will discover that in embracing oneness and letting go of our individual selves, we will be able to see that when one person is starving, we are, in fact, all starving. It is through our empathy at this heightened vibrational frequency that we will teach people how to cope with this overwhelming emotion. As this collective sensitivity grows stronger, it is the psychics of the here and now who, as the spiritual leaders and teachers, will be able to explain to the others exactly what to expect and exactly how this heightened awareness can be achieved. The psychics will help to open people's eyes, by letting them know that the things they perceive to be abnormal are strictly normal to the rest of us. We are fast coming to a point in our lives when the sceptics are really going to have to prove that psychic ability doesn't exist.

To live without judgement is the highest vibrational frequency you can conceive, and yet it is the furthest away from our reality as it stands, for we currently live in a world of judgement that causes wars, fears and battles. When we finally live without judgement there will be no need for forgiveness because all of these things are actually variants of exactly the same thing. That's all the world is – every physical piece of matter that is inside of me can be found somewhere else, we are all linked and a part of the oneness. Everything that was, and everything that is, is all part of the same thing. In truth, there is really no such thing as progression, there is only the realisation that we are already progressed. The trick is to wake up, and break out of the frequency that we are in, which creates this world as an illusion. We are getting close to it, and some people have actually managed to achieve it in this lifetime. Some people are very close and create apports through their thoughts.

At some point, the walls that keep us safe and secure in the knowledge that this world is so real and solid will come crashing down. We will suddenly see, with exceptional clarity, that the perception we have of this world is all one complete illusion and we will go back to knowing ourselves as being forms of energy and feeling ourselves as a consciousness. Having a link to a higher level of consciousness will bring that time about in your own reality an awful lot quicker. It's almost like a moment of coming home. It's a moment when you suddenly see that none of this is real, and none of our fears are valid. The things that appear to have such an effect on us, in reality make little difference to us. All that we are actually experiencing is an assault course in order for us to understand through our feelings.

You are living a virtual reality in a physical world. When you wake up from this virtual reality, you'll be in a different space and vibration. Admittedly, that different space is be very difficult for us to conceive at the moment; but if you imagine it just to be sound, and that sound is light, then that is what it is to be in that space. Even in the spirit world, the spirits still believe that they once lived. So in the spirit world, people's spirits can't tell you what is happening, whether or not they've met Jesus, Buddha, God or Mohammed. They cannot tell you what they're waiting for. They may choose to come back and be reincarnated into this lifetime, or any other lifetime in the past or future, but this is just a loop that is, in fact, going in no direction at all. We believe that we're going through a progressive state when, in actual fact, we're not progressing anywhere.

There is only one progression, and it is not moving forwards, as to move forwards is to still be moving around the earth, instead it is to just move upwards. Everything in nature screams this out to you; the world is round, the oxygen cycle, the nutrition cycle, everything is a cycle. The way to break out of the cycle is just to go up. We see God to be above us, so by going up and being more like God – in other words, light – we are raising your vibrational frequency. We are going up by stepping off the treadmill of life, death and re-birth, and by recognising that we are an energy force, that we are oneness with God, and that there is no separation between spirit and ourselves. There is no separation; we are just light in a physical body and we can make that light stronger. We can move away from the belief that everything in the physical life is real. Think of it like this: you don't have an identity as there is no need for it, you are just light, you are just love, you are divine.

You are moving closer to this but do not see yourself as progressing closer to this, because all that is happening is that you are waking up from a very, very deep slumber. Once awake, will you be truly awake to the fact that you have been asleep? Or will you believe that it is a progression on from the same thing? Will you actually believe that it's another chapter within the same dream? This awakening needs to come from the recognition of the fact that all of this has been created by you as a masked consciousness. By tuning into the Akashic records, the consciousness records, you will discover the purpose of your physical lives, as well as the purpose of the lives you have had in the spirit world. Once you understand the purpose of your existence, you will realise that it is, in truth, without purpose. There truly has been no purpose towards this except to experience that which is ‘not’ in order to appreciate what ‘is’.

When you have the true sense and sensibility of what the truth is, namely that the truth is only light and love, you’ll have the biggest grin and the biggest laugh that you’ve ever had. It’s like walking into a room and wondering why you went in there; you know that you went in for something, and remembering it again makes you laugh at yourself for realising how foolish you’ve been. Never again will you judge yourself or be cross at yourself for something you did, because you will see it as having been a journey through an ‘unreality’, a journey from which you have finally come home after having been lost: I was blind, now I can see. You will see yourself as being in a position where you finally know the truth is not what you see, feel, sense, taste and touch.

Removing blocks

Certain aspects of who you are can get in the way of your psychic talent. Removing blocks not only makes it easier for you to help people, but also adds a sense of fulfilment to your own life.

For example, I used to care too much about what people thought of me. When I was young we moved to different towns, up and down England. If you were going to get on in school it was important that you had friends and people who liked you. I was always the new girl, so I would have to be twice as nice, or more interesting or more generous than everybody else, in order to be taken into a well-established friendship group. As an adult I had taken that need to be liked with me. This need will often create the opposite effect, for if you are concentrating on not being liked, that is what you create.

I was unaware of this aspect of myself, but once I realised it, I saw it show up in every area of my life: the reason I wanted to be a psychic, the fact I had been with men I didn’t want to be with, abusive friendships I stuck with, even down to wanting to be an actress.

At one point in my life I wanted to have my own psychic radio show. I did what I knew worked and I manifested the show through my thoughts. I got in contact with a radio station who said they would give me a slot if I found a sponsor, and in turn, I met Caroline at one of my workshops who said she would help me find a sponsor. It then looked like we could have the show as part of Caroline's company and everything was moving forward – but at a snail's pace, as by this time it was two years on from the first meeting. Caroline and I, by now working together on the project, hired BBC radio presenter Chris Hawkins, pretty much for a job that didn't yet exist. The blow came soon after that, when Caroline said it would take her another year to be ready. I wanted to cry, but I knew I was the 'block' and I asked spirit to show me why the show wasn't happening. The next day the radio station sent me an e-mail saying they could take the show on without the sponsorship.

That's when my training by spirit began. The show was due on in three months time so it was an intense course, but one I had requested. During this time, all sorts of friends suddenly fell out with me over the silliest of misunderstandings. For everything that happened I thought I was to blame, but then it would become clear that that wasn't the case at all. This was my lesson in self-faith and letting go of what others thought of me.

The crunch point came when I ended up falling flat on my back in a café one day. I remember skidding so slowly and so far that I could have grabbed a prawn sandwich in my teeth as I passed by. The noise alone as I hit the floor made the full café gasp! Normally I would have got up, checked to see if anyone I knew had seen me, walked out with my head up and burst into tears! But instead, I simply went to the bar and explained that someone else might fall and did they have a cloth for the grease? I then got a coffee and left. It was only when I was thinking I should have got a free coffee that I realised that I didn't care. I wasn't hurt, there wasn't a mark on me. This was spirit's work, and if I still now cared about other people's opinion of me, I wouldn't be able to do the radio show, as some of the text and e-mails sent to the show are rude and hateful. I see that when you challenge someone's belief they will react against you. I am not bothered! It's the most liberating feeling.

Exercise: Unblocking

Ask spirit what it is that blocks you from a certain work. And ask spirit why the block stops you from reaching the most amazing psychic skills and living the most spiritual life. Keep a diary of events and your blocks will soon become clear. When you know the issue, see it as a block you are already over, as if it was a holding point that, once acknowledged, is then released.

Also, you MUST remember to follow coincidences set out for you, and even if something that you fear comes up, DO IT! This will set you free.

I even became vegetarian with the help of spirit, as I couldn't put meat in my aura due to the harm I could see it was doing to my vibration. The only trouble was that when spirit let go of the vibration I was on, I went back to eating meat.

Seeing oneness

If you really want to be happy and live the best life, you must start to see yourself in everything around you. When we judge others and make them out to be wrong, this only comes back on ourselves. If you want to be happy, see yourself in everything and everyone: 'There I go being homeless; there I am cleaning windows; there go I in that very nice car.'

Find acceptance when things go wrong and know that it is impossible for something to go wrong. If something appears to goes wrong, it may be a disappointment, but you can't know that what you wanted would have been the right thing. Have you ever seen something in a shop and bought it for its beauty, only to get it home and find it doesn't look the same in your lighting? Things look different when we are not living them. Trust the universe to know best.

Exercise: Meditation of expansion

It might be easier to record the steps given here, so that you don't have to read the instructions when practising the exercise.

Take a moment to focus on your breathing. Once you are relaxed, slowly breathe in a bright version of your favourite colour. Then, as you breathe out, release a paler version of the same colour. You are breathing in positive energy and breathing out what doesn't serve you.

Soon you become full of the possible, and you find you are breathing the same colour in and out, and seeing your whole body full of positive energy. Soon the whole room is full of this colour.

You feel your aura start to expand, until it is as big as the area you are sitting in. Breathe again and you expand like a balloon getting bigger until you take up the space in the whole room. The more you breathe, the more you expand, until you find that the whole building you are in is inside you. See yourself expanding until the town, the country and the whole world is inside you.

The more you breathe, the more you expand, until you see yourself with the whole universe inside you.

This is the truth, you are not in your body, your body is in you; you are not in the world, the world is in you; and you are not in the universe, the universe is in you. You are an aspect of God.

Know that you are holding the right perspective. Nothing is separate from you, everything is a whole. Now see yourself back on your chair, but know yourself to be at one with all things.

Bring you attention back into the room and open your eyes.

Going into the Akashic records

We have talked a little about the Akashic records. These are the fonts of knowledge of all things past and all things possible in the future. The records can be see through meditation in the form of visualisation. To gather the same information, you can also travel the time lines, just as with shamanic journeying, which is also a form of visualisation. Going into the Akashic records is a very personal process, so rather than describe my experience, I would ask you to go and see for yourself.

Set out a meditation of intent. Ask your spirit guide to accompany you in the same way as a friend might when you are visiting their home town for the first time. Allow yourself to walk the time lines and the great halls in any way you feel drawn to do. Once you have had this experience you may want to bring this information to other people in your life.

Start by using psychometry. Hold an object that belongs to your client. Ask to be shown that person's past life and have the intent in your heart of seeing anything from that past life that blocks them in this life. Tell the person of the clairvoyant visions you are experiencing. You may see an event or situation that is causing the person to behave in a certain way in this life. For instance, you might discover that someone starved in a past life, which is making them over-eat in this life, resulting in a weight problem. Or you may see that someone has taken a vow of celibacy in a past life, which is causing problems in this life. In such a situation, ask the client if they would like this healed and if they say yes, then ask spirit to send light, love and understanding to heal this lifetime. There may need to be some Karma in this lifetime still to be resolved, but this will happen more quickly when you have done the healing work.

You may find that the person you are healing loses weight, or becomes better at making money, or they may begin to form more fulfilling relationships. On many occasions, simply knowing where a problem comes from is what heals it.

If the client is frightened about healing the block, ask to be shown in this life and the next where this situation will take the client. You may see an event that will heal the situation, or you may see the situation getting worse or carrying on through many incarnations. Always allow the person you are healing the free will to decide what they want, even if you think that's not the best for the client.

Don't be shocked if you find lifetimes on other planets. Some of us have had past lives in other solar systems, while some of us may have future lives on them. Yes, you too could have been an alien, and you may now be thinking that it explains one or two things about you! Be very careful how you explain this to the client, not everyone is open to the idea of being an alien, and too many of us have had this viewpoint influenced by Star Trek and War of the Worlds; my personal favourite is Doctor Who!

When you relay information from the Akashic records, you may find your client was already conscious of it on some level.

The more time you spend in meditation on this level, the more you will know the difference between Akashic information and the imagination.

Time lines

Many shamans believe they can walk time lines through journeying. As time isn't linear, I personally see time to be a web of opportunity of our own making.

When it comes to reincarnation I believe we can go backwards into the lifetimes of certain historical figures, almost like a 'walk in' spirit who is there to observe the intentions behind the decisions of the historical figures. This, I believe, is reserved for very enlightened spirits who would be able to see the person with compassion, without judgement and wouldn't jump in to change the events of the past. For example, if you wanted to know what it was like to be Winston Churchill, or even Adolf Hitler, in order to understand something more clearly, you might live through the whole or aspects of their lifetime. Some people believe that they, as a spirit, walked into someone else's body. This would have been at a time when the original spirit was about to die, perhaps due to an accident or illness in the physical body. When I talk to people who believe they are 'walk ins', they say they have no memory of their childhood, and they also tell me that members of their family have commented on how different they have been since the life-threatening incident occurred. So, when we reincarnate can we go both forwards and backwards into the lifetimes of other physical bodies? We are powerful creative beings, and I believe we make our future, learning the lessons along the way.

PART FOUR

GOING PROFESSIONAL

Many psychics hide behind the idea that 'spirit' wants them to do this work, that they have a calling from spirit to work as a psychic and to help people. In truth, spirit wants us to be happy. If this is the work that will make you happy, then do it with all your heart. When I say spirit wants us to be happy, there is a very good reason for this. If we are happy then we send out light vibration, whereas if we are unhappy we don't. So spirit looks for the right job for the person and not the right person for the job. You will never be forced into doing this work as that serves no one. In truth, the calling is coming from you, your higher self. That way you can't blame spirit when there isn't the money coming in or if anything else goes wrong. I often hear people say that they ask spirit for clients, and then when someone in need talks to them on the bus, they wonder why they always attract mad people. Your clients are everybody, whether they pay or not. Your job isn't to give everyone readings but to offer everyone love, and if you are not full of love yourself then it becomes very hard to give.

However, some people will have a certain attitude or be hurtful to you, which makes them very hard to love. Here I will discuss client tips, which will help you to see the beauty and innocence in all people.

I strongly advise you to first get some training in counselling and especially grief counselling. I did this type of training as a volunteer, working with people with drug-related HIV. This type of counselling was called Buddying. The Healthy Options Team (HOT) in Mile End, London, gave me the training I needed to work as a psychic which, apart from being very enjoyable, showed me how to care for my clients without taking the work home with me. Once I've given a reading, I forget all about it until the client comes to see me again, which is great as I never need to worry that I won't keep someone's confidence.

The more varied life experience you have, and the more contact you have with different cultures and walks of life, the better you will be in your work. The greatest boon to this is that you will have a really interesting life!

You will find tend to find that the people who come and see you are going through the same problems that you have personally experienced or have experienced through loved ones. Spirit is then able to use less energy as it doesn't have to let you know how each client is feeling, by giving you their emotions and the fears, because you will have already experienced them yourself and will be full of understanding. For instance, in my life I have worked in theatre and, because I understand the stresses of that area of work, many of my clients include people who are related to the media. I once had a crack- and heroin-addicted boyfriend (who is now clean and happy), so I have an insight into that troubled world, and now many of my clients are family members of such sufferers, and sometimes, but not often, I see the actual addicts themselves. The addicts appear less often because they avoid the people who can really help them until they are ready to face the problem.

I have travelled around the world and met travellers and people from all over the world, especially from India and Pakistan. This really helps to give me an understanding of each client's situation. You need to truly appreciate, for instance, that a young man from the Philippines in his twenties or thirties who still lives at home is adhering to a totally different lifestyle to someone from the USA who lives in the fast lane.

The client and you

When you are giving help and advice to people, it's easy to start to see yourself as being more 'aware' or 'in tune' than your clients, for they will always mirror an aspect of you. You must never believe that you are above anyone that you are helping. You are not giving someone a hand up, but a hand along. Sometimes, your clients may want to put you on a pedestal, in which case give thanks, but don't be tempted on to the stool as it's a long fall, and spirit will be there to teach you a lesson. You cannot do the work from above, only from the side.

I would ask you to see your clients as an amazing creative force for their own lives. It is your job is to remind them that they are that amazing creative force.

Every client is different, but, even so, people can be bracketed into character types. Some of the funniest comedy shows are hilarious to us because we know a person who is just like the one on our screens – we recognise the type. My fear is that what I am about to tell you may look judgemental on my part. It's not a judgement, as I don't view my clients as good or bad, I would only like to share with you what I have observed in people over the years. In truth, recognising traits in people is useful for any type of work.

When I first started as a psychic medium, people who came to visit me just gave me donations, and I relied on my theatre work for proper wages. Over a period of time, I began to get more and more people coming to visit me for my psychic work. I also noticed that the donations were getting bigger and I began to feel that it was time to start charging for my time – and, anyway, I was finding it difficult to hold down what was fast becoming two jobs. By the time I was charging, I had paid for my psychic education and I was getting so many readings it was stopping me from having a life of my own.

Being in a spiritual field, people will expect you to work for free. Sometimes people send out e-mails to every address in the 'Psychic Directory' (addresses listed in the back of this book) asking for free help. In their message, they say that they feel that the psychic is the only person who can help them, and sometimes they test the psychic by asking them to name their dead relative.

At first, I always responded to these e-mails, but I soon found that I was spending all my time answering the messages. I found I was becoming annoyed and exhausted by it; of course this was my own doing, but it's hard to know if someone really does need your help or not. Another difficulty is that you can damage your reputation for being spiritual if you are not permanently on tap for free advice. But I have thought up a way of dealing with this problem and I am happy to share this secret with you. Of course, by telling you my secret I will lose the ability to use it for myself, but I am stronger now and am able to say no to people, or do nothing at all. So, try my scheme if you find you are overwhelmed by calls for help.

I invented a personal assistant, called Emma. I then created a standard e-mail, giving details on how to book an appointment, which I sent out from Emma whenever anyone randomly wrote in asking for advice. In this way, it looked as if my PA received the message and passed it on to me. Hardly anyone made an appointment, so my e-mails were reduced drastically.

I now have a real PA for five hours a week to help me cope with the workload, but what was interesting about this was how quickly you can cosmically order something without even trying. My new PA really is called Emma too!

As a psychic, you can't be seen to be unspiritual. I don't have all the time in the world, but many people think that psychics just love their job and will give up all their time to do readings for nothing, whereas no one would usually expect to ask a trained solicitor for advice without getting a bill at the end of it; it is rare to find any kind of professional using their gift to help people without expecting to get paid.

I had always done mediumship in exchange for a gift rather than money, but this became unmanageable when I didn't have enough to live on and I was turning down paid readings to make the time for sittings. Now I only do mediumship as part of a reading.

Many of you reading this may have difficulty in accepting what I am saying here. Anyone who wanted to help people would do so free of charge, wouldn't they? Indeed, we do all the time. The overall question is 'Why should psychics charge for their gifts from God'? This is easily answered – because many have trained long and hard to gain their gifts and everyone has a basic right to have enough money to live on. The dense energy that judgemental people send psychics and mediums for earning a living does more harm than the money earned.

Client variation

There are few jobs in the world where you get to know people so intimately. It is wonderful to be able to know people in this way, but as many times as you meet great people, you will also meet difficult ones, sometimes from the same stock and area of life. Each client is an individual, but here are guidelines on the type of client you may meet.

The 'me' syndrome

When a person seeks advice they often come with a 'me' problem. A 'me' problem comes from the belief that we are separate from each other and that there is lack in the world, and due to the feeling that there isn't enough to go round they feel it is they who will miss out. The 'me' doesn't realise that all of these problems come from the decisions made regarding themselves as people. One of the most common problems I have seen during my readings is women who are in a loveless relationship, only staying there because the clock is ticking and they want children. This is a truth for them, the truth being that yes, the clock is ticking, but the decision to stay with their existing partner comes from a belief that there is a lack of relationship opportunity for them. If they were coming from a position of trust and power then they would know that they could find the right relationship at any time. Many of us will know the sensation of meeting someone and feeling that we have known them our whole lives. Being with someone who doesn't understand us at all creates the opposite feeling. The little 'me' isn't empowered. A psychic has the ability to turn around 'me' into 'em – power'.

If a person comes for a reading with a 'me' problem, then by the time they leave they should have turned that around to 'em'.

Case study: The fostering company

Two friends had appointments to see me. The woman who came in to see me first had a charity for fostering children and I immediately liked her very much. She lived for her daughter and her work, but this wasn't bringing in the money and put her in a most difficult situation. I felt a bit of media backing would help her company and we talked of ways in which I could use my contacts in the media to spread the word about her company. I didn't charge her for the hour we spent together and she left the reading with a more positive outlook, and full of hope.

The second woman, her friend, who was also her business partner, then came in. She was negative from the start and responded in an argumentative way to the smallest suggestions. I know that the two women had talked to each other in-between the readings, and her friend would have told her I hadn't charged her for the hour. Towards the end of the reading, the woman said she felt no clearer on what to do and I responded by saying that it was fine not to pay me for the reading, but she still gave me twenty pounds. How two women driven by the same passion could be so different in energy and in politeness was very confusing. This left me feeling hurt and not wanting to put their business forward with my media friend. For one person you would give the earth, whilst for the other not even the time of day.

The 'yes, but…' client

This person will be deeply in pain. They feel the world has failed them and now you, a psychic, will also fail them. They have tried everything to make their life better but there is nothing you can say that will change their situation. They have come to hear a prediction for a happy future, but one that they do not want to take any responsibility for. If you don't do what they want, and you do the work that will do them the most good, that is to try to inspire, the likelihood is you will lose the battle. This type of client may even become angry with you.

Spirit doesn't often show up to these appointments because there isn't much point as the client wants to add the appointment to their list of failures. If you have the energy for it, try your best for these people. You will most likely feel drained and need a big energy clearing in the room after the appointment. I often advise this type of client to read certain books and don't charge them for the appointment. I give them about fifteen minutes in which I ask them to just play along with what I am about to tell them, as if they were watching a film. Although they are only observing, my aim is to get them immersed in 'the film' with the hope that they might absorb or respond to the positive angle of my words. However, usually they have made a decision on what they will get out of the reading before they even arrive, and it is impossible to get past that block.

Ask Spirit to give the client the wake up call they need and tell them about the following books: *The Power of Intention* by Wayne W. Dyer and *Ask and it is Given* by Jerry and Esther Hicks both published by Hay House.

The obsessive relationship addict

Case study: Facing a break-up

The first psychic fair I ever attended was at the Chelsea Town Hall. It was a big event and I saw seventeen clients that day.

One woman who sat in front of me, interrupted me after two minutes and said she was only interested in hearing about one thing, and that was her relationship. I didn't see her in a relationship, and she said she wasn't in one. I explained again that I didn't do future predictions, but all she wanted to hear was about her ex-boyfriend. But I couldn't see a break-up. She got annoyed and said, 'Tell me what you see,' so I talked about her career.

She said yes to everything I was saying, then insisted I went back to look at relationships. Again I said I couldn't see anyone around her. She said he was in America. It turned out she hadn't even been in touch with her 'ex' for two years and she was asking me to spy on his life. Does he think of me? Has he met someone else? What is he doing? Is he happy without me?

At that point I stopped the reading and she reacted by telling me I was a useless psychic and a disappointment, since if I was any good I would have been able to see him, as he was all she thought about. She was keeping the relationship alive by using psychics to give her new things to think about in regard to this person.

I was very hurt by this reading and I even played back the tape again to see if there was anything I could have done to avoid what happened. But I decided I had done everything within my power to help the woman.

Six months later it was my first day working in an esoteric shop in London. Ever since I had come across the shop I had wanted to work there as a reader, and I was so happy to have achieved my goal. My first client had gone well; I went up to the shop floor to collect my second client, only to find it was the same woman from the psychic fair in Chelsea. I rushed her downstairs so that we didn't have the conversation on the shop floor in front of my new boss. Once we were downstairs, she told me how sorry she was about the last time we had met. She said I had finally made her wake up to the truth – which was that the relationship was over. I then gave her a great reading with which she was happy, and the blot on my track record was cleared.

I don't know of anyone who hasn't had an obsessive love. However, a client may go from psychic to psychic to talk about something their friends are sick of hearing about. Sometimes a psychic will make this mental disorder worse by saying things like, 'I see him coming back to you. Yes, he is thinking of you, he regrets leaving you, he's thinking of having children with you.' Being a psychic means you can tune into what people *want* to hear which can possibly leave the person mentally unwell. This is a big responsibility and must not be taken lightly.

Don't allow the client to use you as a way of staying connected with the person they are obsessing over, which is simply causing them not to move on.

Questions which are ok: Did he/she ever love me? Where did we go wrong? How can I move on?

Questions to watch out for: Does he or she love their partner? Are they only with them for the kids? Is he/she coming back?

There will be great pressure on you to answer these questions, but know that if you do answer them, you are only adding to the things flying around in their head late at night. Many will want to know if this person was a soul mate, thinking that this will mean the relationship was meant to be, and that by not being together, somehow something is wrong in the universe.

Although these clients may not seem fragile, beware, as these thoughts can turn into an obsession which a person may never get over, never being able to move on. An obsession can prevent the client from getting into another relationship, and it can even turn them into a stalker.

You will usually encounter this type of client on phone lines. When they can't control their own anxiety over the loss of a person, a large phone bill is a small price to pay for keeping the relationship alive through talking about it.

The non-sceptic, sceptic

You will recognise this person from one of their first sentences: 'I believe in what you people do.' For a start, if you do truly believe, then you wouldn't need to say it in the first place, but this statement is about winning you on to their side, the clue being in the 'you people'.

The reading will start off fine. But this client believes they know how a psychic should work and what psychic 'powers' are, meaning that they won't be able to interpret the information due to being very 'left-brained', and will need the information to be put across by your left brain. It is likely that they are looking for a cold reading, and are putting up energy blocks. We will talk more on blocked readings later.

The blind believer

It is hard to empower this person as they will believe in anything you say, but not in themselves. They normally want to know what is going to happen in the future and quite often this will feel like a very bland reading, as they may have very little going on in their life for you to get your teeth into. You may wonder why they have come to see you as their life seems to be ticking along with nothing much going wrong; it just is what it is.

But they have come to see you to add some spice into their life and whatever you say is going to happen in the future, so they will get excited or worry about it. The problem is, they are not creating their own future. At this point you could create their future for them by telling them a fantastic story about how their life is going to change, and the chances are they will then go away and make this happen. Due to all thoughts being creative, they will send out for this to come into their lives. However, the psychist is then interfering with another's free will.

A good question to ask is, 'What are you doing when you like yourself the most?' instead of 'What do you enjoy doing?' Find out what brings them growth. The chances are they won't be able to answer the question, but it will get them thinking along the right lines. Life doesn't happen to you, you happen to life, and there is no life without creative thought. Inspire creative thought and you will have changed a person's life into being what they want it to be, not what you have created for them.

My friend was fooled, but I won't be

This person comes for a reading because their friend recommended you to them. They may not themselves need a reading and have come with one purpose in mind: they're jealous of the influence you have over their friend, and they want to reveal you as a fraud. This is the same as a sceptic coming to you, but there is more at stake as all the healing you did for their friend is at risk. As in the case for the sceptic's reading, you can't refuse to read for them (as this would seem that you were incapable of 'cold reading' them), but they will block your readings as much as they can, which in turn will only block their own life. The trick is to offer to describe something in their home; their sofa is a good item to choose. The person will hopefully say, 'OK, but what's that got to do with a reading?' You can then ask them if they feel that being able to visualise a sofa that you have never seen is a sign of being psychic. Of course they can't say no, and then you can add, 'So now that you can see I have psychic ability, I would like to read for you.' The blocks that they have put up will then fall away, as there is no need for them. You can now really help this person to deal with their fears. Their friend recommended you to them for a reason, now you have to get on with the job.

I come without a purpose, I just want to know what you see for me

This person may also come via word of mouth, or because they had a great reading with you in the past.

This is like going to the dentist for a check-up and finding there is nothing wrong with your teeth; there is no work for the dentist to do. Often a person will come to see a psychic for a check-up. 'Am I on the right path? Am I missing something?'

If there is little in the way of a problem for you to work with, then the reading will feel bland for you and the client, but remember that the client is leaving with something very valuable, namely reassurance that they are alright. Be sure to make this point as clear as you can. This reading can be difficult if you have to fill an hour, especially if you're working in a place where you can't charge for parts of an hour. How I deal with this is to give the information in fifteen minutes and not charge for the reading. This is a loss of money for you and the place you are working in, but if you do waffle on about nothing for an hour, you run the risk of getting a bad reputation both for yourself and for the place where you're working.

I want to know what the future holds for me

The risk here is to start giving future predictions. After a while you can become so worn down you can't keep up the fight for truth. On my website, my fliers and on every piece of information about me, it says I don't give future predictions. Yet I will still be asked – after all, that is what people believe a psychic does. This is our own fault for if you look at the back of magazines or surf the Internet, you will be confronted with large claims of 'accurate future predictions'. I'm not saying that you can't predict the future, but the future isn't set in stone. I get clairvoyant visions of the future from spirit that are always accurate and are for the purpose of inspiring the client into making the move or the jump they need to make at that moment in time. The intention is always to inspire action rather than to encourage the person to just sit back and wait. I get most visions for clients who will do their own thing and not take my word for it, for people who know their own mind. So, the irony is that the people who want the predictions most are the people I am least likely to see visions for.

At the start of a reading, I advise you to ask people what they want to get out of the reading. This way you will know what and whom you are dealing with, and from the offset you will be able to explain clearly to the client what you do. You don't want to know what questions they are going to ask, just what they want to get out of the reading. Someone might say clarity or communication with someone in spirit, or advice on a relationship or work issue. They may also say 'I want to know my future', and then you can advise them when the fairground is coming to town…

I always let the client know why I won't predict the future. It's harder when you have a spontaneous vision during the reading, because after that, the person will expect more visions in answer to their questions. I can't create a vision, they simply come to me. If I create a vision, it's my imagination. If I try to force it, I will simply imagine for the client whatever it is that I know they want to hear, which is then a lie and also disempowering. In this case, a client is handing over their power to you; they are giving you the power to make decisions for them, which is not a good situation for either of you as when it goes wrong they end up blaming you.

Case study: Telling the truth

One client who kept insisting I told her the future even used her son as a bargaining tool. 'It's not for me, it's for my son. He's being bullied at school and I was wondering if the solicitor will help us to win the case so that he can move to a different school.' I explained I couldn't say whether or not the case would be won, but that I felt the solicitor was a good woman. She was surprised that I could see the solicitor was a woman, so she was really happy with what I said.

A few weeks later I came home to a message on my answer-phone saying, 'Becky, I just wanted to let you know how disappointed I was with the reading. You told me the solicitor would be good for my son's case, but you were wrong as she has been taken off the case because she is moving office.'

I'm glad I didn't take the call. The solicitor was good for the case; I hadn't told the client that the solicitor would win the case, or that she would even be taking the case up until the end, because I didn't know!

Never be afraid to say, 'I don't know'. It will inspire faith in everything else you say – and we don't, and can't, know everything.

Business or career person

I like these clients; it's a very easy reading. You can tune into the people around this person to see if they are good people and how they all relate with one another. Good business is about good relationships, so your job on this one is making sure that the right people get together.

You can also save someone a lot of time and money. One of my first ever readings was for a couple who were travelling on a cruise ship where I was reading tarot cards. On one of the cards, I kept being drawn to some grapes. Looking at the grapes, I had a horrible sense of foreboding, which I relayed to the couple. As I gave them the information, I tried to decipher what it meant, wondering if it could possibly mean they were drinking too much wine. I glanced up to see two gaping mouths. Only an hour before they had had a business meeting with a couple who wanted them to invest in a vineyard. The wife then turned to her husband and said, 'I told you it wasn't a good idea!'

If there are decisions in business to be made, ask the client to put them in number order, then tune into each number in turn and describe what the situation is without knowing what it is. This way you won't allow your own thoughts to influence the reading.

For example: A: Buy a house in town, B: Rent a house in the country, or C: Buy a house abroad.

Ask for each option to be written on a separate piece of paper. Hold each piece of paper without being able to read it; see which one feels better. All of this will impress the client and show them that the right answer is coming from spirit and not from you.

You may also pick up on the client's wish, which would be ideal, as the things a person wants to do normally work out best. People often fear that their ideas won't work out, and that the future is outside of their control, leading them to block what their heart is saying. You can hear a person's heart and empower them to follow it.

Life-changing crossroads

This is something I hear every day, 'I just think I'm at a bit of a crossroads'. Often the person isn't at a crossroads at all, but has just become bored with the road they are on. A bit of spice and excitement may be the only revamp that is needed. Most of us believe we have to make a big change when we feel that something is lacking in our life, much like being really hungry and thinking we need a large meal. However, sometimes when we are hungry all we really need is a glass of water. Go with your own belief in the client's situation, not their belief, and see what's missing for them.

I don't want to hear anything bad

This person may have been spooked by tales of psychics giving clients bad news; they may have heard that a psychic told someone when they were going to die, or that they were going to be involved in a car crash. This is another good reason to avoid giving a future prediction.

When I used tarot cards for readings, I found that one of the problems was that the vivid pictures on the cards sometimes gave the client the wrong impression. For instance, if a person asked about a relationship and the three of swords showed up, the client would instantly think the relationship was about to fall apart – the card depicts a heart with three swords running through it. It was then hard to explain that this doesn't always imply bad news. Some of the worst relationships we experience make us grow in the best ways, for we can't **live** life by avoiding pain. What a psychic can do is offer a new positive insight into the worst disappointment. Many people consult a psychic to avoid pain, but these people need to be empowered to know they can handle it. The above statement, 'I don't want to hear anything bad,' comes from a place of lack of faith within you. If the person who said these words had faith, they would know they could change anything bad that came up in their life.

However, it is the responsibility of the psychic to make sure nothing sounds like bad news in a reading. Never finish a reading on a negative note.

Case study: The nice watch

While teaching a class on psychometry, I was telling my students how important it was to end every reading on a positive note. I gave them an example of what I meant. One of my students was holding a woman's watch and he said he could feel emotions of depression and sadness rising up from it. He felt that the owner of the watch wasn't at all happy and was at their lowest point. I asked him to end this information with something positive; he said, 'It's a nice watch!'

Different cultures

Every culture has its own mystics, and your job as a psychic medium will be viewed differently by each culture. A Catholic friend of mine from the Philippines once asked to see my tarot deck and as he looked at the cards the devil card fell on the floor. He freaked out, believing he was cursed. I had to explain that the card had appeared because of his complicated relationships with women, nothing too sinister, but because of his religious upbringing, he believed psychics worked with the devil. The Church and ruling authorities have always seen the influence of the mystic seers over the masses as a threat to their control, and have consequently tried to instill a fear of the power of mysticism into the people. The witch hunts of the past are proof of this.

Different cultures also produce different energy levels. For example, Americans tend to have large energy because the USA is a huge place, and you can be big there without too much of a problem.

People from some cultures are very pushy, and will try to make you move your appointments around them. Some cultures hold no respect for what you do and are very suspicious; others hold great respect for psychic work, almost too much.

One man who visited me didn't believe me when I said I couldn't contact his grandfather; he kept saying, 'For me he will come,' and offering me more money to bring him forward. This is often a problem with mediumship, if a spirit doesn't step forward, rather than believing that the spirit doesn't want to talk to them, the client will believe you are hiding something!

It is important to understand a bit about every culture. I once got into trouble in Pakistan for mentioning a past life during Ramadan; the people I was with took offence because it's not part of the Islamic belief. Perhaps if I had mentioned it any other time, my words would have been acceptable and not disrespectful.

In Asian countries, such as Vietnam, the Philippines or Thailand, it is normal for people to continue to live at home with their parents after the age of thirty. Yet in the Western World, we might try to inspire them to move out, thinking they live their life through fear of moving on and having their own independence.

Read up as much as you can, and call on spirit to help you along the path. As long as you see with an open eye during readings, you will find you can blend with any person without separation.

Ascended masters, angels and aliens

The more the vibration of the planet is changing, the more people are waking up. These 'waking people' are the clients who come to see you, but do not know why.

At this time, more than any other, there are now more people who are born with very strong psychic abilities. These children are called indigo children. Many of whom are grown up and ready to start work with high level masters in the spirit world. They have come back to help with the change, but, like the rest of us, they may also feel lost and homesick from time to time.

There are angels who, although they may never have had wings and been in the angelic realm, still have that angelic sensitivity. When you meet these people they are normally very beautiful and have a spiritual glow about them. Often, they are having difficulty with life on a global level and will ask questions like: 'Why can't everybody live in peace?'; 'Why does this person in my life hate me so much?' Some may judge these people as being wet behind the ears and a bit gullible, but with such innocence coming out of them, you can't fail to want to give them a hug and put them on a white fluffy cloud.

We humans are happy to believe that just because something isn't physical, it doesn't exist. Of course, in my belief, this simply isn't true. We are energy, like everything around us. In fact, we humans are the odd energy out, simply because we are physical. Following this line of thought, is it not possible that there is non-physical life on other planets? If that is the case, is it not also possible that the non-physical life form may incarnate into a human physical body? Some aliens are being born to an earth life for the first time, after having lived other lives on other planets. They are often very lost and in need of lots of guidance; they do not need to hear the psychic saying, 'Hey, you were an alien in your last life!' as this could come as a bit of a shock. I have to say I haven't met very many reincarnated beings so far, but the ones I have come across were very pleasant.

Maybe 'aliens' are watching us go through this time of change. Maybe one day we will be able to communicate with them, once we come out of this dense vibration of fear we currently live in. If they were to come now, we would most likely kill them. They need to wait until we can truly understand, and some of them have come here with no memory of who they are in order to try and help us come to terms with their arrival. This might all seem a bit hard to believe, but nothing in this world is solid, even though it may seem so. You will know these 'aliens' when you meet them; they just won't seem to fit in.

Friends and relatives: privacy protection

A person may want a reading to find out information about somebody close to them. They may be worried about a member of the family, or want to know how a partner feels about them. A client may come with no personal problem to speak of for themselves and therefore no personal need for the reading, but you can feel the worry and fear coming off them. I have sometimes been stumped when looking into someone's life and seeing no problems for them, but then I have realised that the problems are with everyone else around them. This type of person will often live their lives through others, as sometimes happens with a mother and her children. It is then not possible to give them the type of reading they desire. It is very easy to look in and describe what a person looks like, be that a family member, a friend or a partner, but then someone asks you about 'John' and you see nothing. Spirit will show me a 'no entry' sign, meaning that the person being discussed has a privacy clause. This could indicate that the person is very private, or is someone who would hate the idea of being discussed by a stranger, let alone by a psychic.

Whenever this comes up I don't push for information, no matter how much the client may feel they need to know. Sometimes this information could be the whole reason they booked the reading: they just want to know 'Does he love me?' It is the spirit guide of the person being discussed that will block the information in order to protect the person that is their charge. It simply wouldn't be polite for you to do a reading.

Ask spirit for a 'no entry' clairvoyant sign so you don't waste too much time, trying to read the unreadable.

Late clients and no shows

Everyone runs late from time to time, but a client being late can cause a knock on effect for the rest of your clients. It's tempting to see the client during your break in-between appointments, but it's important not to give up your break because of someone's lateness. You need a fifteen minute break in between every client. If you don't, you won't be able to cleanse your energy and one client will blend into another. When I have held readings in shops, I have sometimes done eight hours of back-to-back readings, the effect being that it doesn't do you or the clients any good. If a client is late, then it should count as their loss of time, not yours, and they should pay for the full appointment, unless there is a very good reason why they were late.

Clients may also not turn up for an appointment. I reckon they think that because you are psychic you will know that they are not coming, and therefore don't even bother to phone to say so. At the point of booking make sure you get a phone number, so you can call a no show. Sometimes they give a false number, or they won't answer the phone. My message goes something like this: '*Hi ***, you have an appointment with me that started 10 minutes ago. I hope you are OK and nothing has happened. Let me know if you need directions. Please could you give me a call, as if you are not coming, so I can go* *and have a cup of tea. Talk to you soon.'*

Never leave a ranting message about how you now can't afford lunch; that might well be the case, especially if you have paid for the room hire to do the reading. A no show can make you very annoyed, but that level of vibration will affect your other readings. Just let it go; there is little you can do. I take it that a no show is spirit's way of saying I needed a break.

Types of reading

Phone readings

A commonly asked question is: 'Are phone readings as accurate as face-to-face readings?'

Sceptics believe many psychics do a thing called cold reading. A cold reader can obtain information about a person by analyzing the person's body language, clothing or fashion, hairstyle, gender, sexual orientation, religion, race or ethnicity, level of education, etc. This technique is also called profiling. I don't think you could do those techniques in a phone reading. A great way to test a psychic is over the phone, for if they have a strong connection with spirit then the reader will have no problem at all.

The beginning of a face-to-face reading does involve an amount of cold reading whilst you are tuning in, but once started, this can lead into the heart of the matter, the issues you couldn't possibly have known. Over the phone you don't usually have as much time to tune into the person and make the connection, although phone readings can be just as accurate as face-to-face meetings. Whenever I do a phone reading on the radio, I have to be on the ball in record time. Sometimes the only information you get from the caller is that they would like a 'general reading'. You must then tune into the area of life with the most fixable problems.

For the best results when doing a phone reading, make sure the following conditions are in place:

Turn off all other phones.

Choose a time when you know you won't be disturbed and inform the client when to ring.

If available, set up a recording machine that records both sides of the conversation (there are some great ones on the market and I strongly advise having one). For legal reasons, you must let the client know you are recording. So when you start recording, state on the tape, 'I am starting the tape now, the date today is: ***.' You may also say, 'This is a reading by *** with ***.' This will give you a professional tone.

Starting the call with these statements also helps to set the boundaries for the call. These boundaries are further kept in place at the end of the call by saying, 'We have five minutes left. Do you have any last questions?' If more questions are put forward and you are running overtime, you can say, 'We are at time now, what is your very final question?' People often assume that you have lots of time to chat. Maybe that is the case and a chat would be nice, but a friendly professionalism will mean you won't be called up at all hours of the night by someone who thinks you won't mind because the two of you are now friends…

Make sure you have a pen ready to take down the client's address.

Always have a glass of water to hand as you might get a dry throat.

Set out tarot cards or whatever you need for your work. Sometimes having a cheque or letter the person sent you for the psychometry is a good idea.

Before the reading, make sure you have meditated or been in silence for at least five minutes. Focus your attention into the here and now by focusing on your breathing. This will help you to leave behind anything connected with your home life.

Don't, during the reading, fiddle with a pen or think you can do your nails. Even when on the radio, people can hear if you are talking to someone else or not concentrating on them, and they can also hear when you are smiling. Start every reading with a smile.

Phone reading payment suggestions

Often a person will want a phone reading on the spot and they will not wait to send you a cheque. It is possible to do a deal with a phone company whereby they charge the client and give you a small percentage of the call cost, but this might encourage you to keep the call going longer.

Many people who phone psychic phone lines can become addicted. Unable to control their own anxiety, they need to talk to the person on the other end of the line to make them feel better. This then forms an addiction, which can run into a great deal of money. If you make the choice to work for these companies, make sure you find one with great integrity – there are some about.

Any psychic who has tried to get a credit card facility will find that the card companies have prejudices against psychics as they believe they will have to make more refunds for unhappy clients. A way to be able to take credit cards is to use Pay Pal, World Pay or other such companies on your website. It's quite simple to set up but can take a few weeks of security checks. I would say that if you are very right brain, as most psychics are, pay a left-brained person who can do it easily for you.

Another payment alternative is to ask people to buy you a gift of your choice from a mail-order company. I have done this in the past as there is always something I need, even if it's tapes for readings. The company sends a receipt to the client and I then do the reading. The items arrive a few days later.

However, the best form of payment I have found is the good old cheque, although that's not to say it doesn't have its problems; I have lost money over bounced cheques in the past. Normally I ask the client to send a cheque to a PO box address, which avoids the problem of having people at your door telling you they had no one else to turn to. Once I receive the cheque I call the client and fix an appointment time.

Remember, if you live with other people, you must consult with them before you launch into this type of work.

E-mail and messenger readings

This is an area that will lose value for the client in terms of accuracy. If someone sends you an e-mail it is possible to tune into that person and send a reply e-mail that answers any questions they have. The only problem is that if you don't get a response, it is hard to see what blocks in the person have put them in the situation they are in.

There will also be a need for exact statement, which is difficult. The question: 'Will my relationship work out?' can only be answered with a 'yes' or 'no'. The most interesting part of that question is why is the person is asking it? Is this a past relationship failure fear? Is it because the person lives overseas and the client would have to change their whole life to be with that person? The deeper answers are the ones which are the most useful in the longer term.

Please bear in mind that typing is a left-brain activity, which might mean that you are blocking the psychic creative ability of the right brain.

Mediumship can also be done by e-mail, bringing a message from the spirit world. However, I would suggest that you reply to the e-mail on a tape and post that to the client as it will make you a better channel. Also, depending on the speed of dictation, you might miss information if you can't type as fast as spirit can convey information.

MSN messenger readings are great. I once did a test reading for the website master and founder of the famous website 'Bad Psychics'. His website is designed to 'out' fraudulent mediums and psychics. The reading went well, with the web master agreeing to the majority of what I had to say. I wouldn't have taken the risk with a renowned sceptic if I hadn't felt that I could be accurate. The benefits of using an Instant Messenger is that there is instant contact with the client, meaning they can ask questions and you can reply, tuning in as you go. If you take this one stage further with video Internet, there are really no limits to reading people all over the world. Now every psychic can describe himself or herself as an international psychic!

Skype, along with a web cam, is another great idea. The client can then see you and hear you at the same time.

Postal readings from a photo

When doing a reading from a photo, where you record your reading on a tape, make sure to ask for a list of questions along with it. I was once asked to read the health of a baby from a photo, but felt that this was too much responsibility for a distance reading; it's advisable to be cautious. Things that can't be asked about in the reading might keep someone awake at night, so make sure you are thorough with the information.

It's a good idea not to look at the photo before the reading, so start the tape and then look at the photo and say what you see. Often it is hard to make these readings fit a time, and if you charge by the minute, people will feel nervous thinking you could be talking for hours. So it's a good idea to have a maximum time, preferably no longer than half an hour.

The psychic tool box

Hopefully you will have taken the time to experiment with various methods for giving a reading. Bear in mind that things like Tarot cards are just tools, and whilst you can find a tool you enjoy using, be reminded that they are like having stabilisers on a bike; once you learn to ride the bike, take the stabilisers off. Many psychics keep them on for fear of falling and failing during a reading. Tools are useful for developing skills, but you must have faith in your gifts in order to progress. Remember that the important message in a reading will always come forward no matter what the tool.

Tarot cards

There are 78 cards, 14 in each of the four suits and 22 major arcana cards. The cards can be read upside down, which would give you the reversed meaning of the card. When you are doing a reading with the cards you are laying out someone's life before them. I feel that if there are more problems and issues than 78 cards the right way up can depict, your client needs more than a reading! These cards are symbolic and can be used to access your inspiration. It takes time to learn what each card means, let alone the layout for a spread. The way I learnt how to use them was by getting rid of the book! Whilst you are trying to remember all of the meanings of the cards you are using your right brain, which is linked to logic, maths and language. The left brain is creativity and inspiration; dyslexic people often make great psychics because of their ability to be more left than right brain.

So, when looking at Tarot cards or any form of reading from inspiration it is important to quieten the right brain.

Exercise: Learning what the Tarot cards mean to you

Take three cards out of the pack at the start of your day. Then read them later in the evening to see if you can work out how the pictures relate to your day. The more you do this the more you will develop a relationship with the cards.

A new Tarot spread

This layout was given to me by spirit when I was beginning the Tarot. Place two cards for the past on the top of the table. Then two cards for the present below those on the table, then place two cards for the future below those and one card on each side of the present cards in the middle, to make a cross shape. These two cards on either side of the present represent what's going on inside your mind. Sometimes, what's on your mind isn't what's going on in your life.

Astrology

Astrology is the study of the movement of the planets and how this affects us according to their relative positions at the time we were born. Split into twelve signs, the sun moves one degree per day, giving twelve sections of a person's personality to draw up into a chart. This subject requires considerable study and I wouldn't even begin to try to explain it in the limited space available here. The same goes for Chinese astrology.

Palmistry

This is the study of the lines on the palms of the hand; the reading also includes looking at the shape of the hands themselves, the length and width of the fingers and the size of the mounds on the palm. Here are some brief guidelines to look out for:

Female hands: Women with long fingers and long palms are sensitive and creative.

A wiry look to the hand, combined with long knotty fingers and a square wide shape, suggests an inquisitive mind and bubbly personality.

Short fingers and a longish palm denote a more impulsive temperament: the hands of true survivors.

Men's Hands: Men with long fingers pay attention to detail, and are focussed on the future.

If the third finger is longer than the index finger, this implies a man with high sexual energy.

Runes

It is said that Odin sat under a tree and meditated, the runes being a product of his meditation. The only thing is, I think it's only Odin who can use the runes! Stones are carved with symbols or letters, each letter having a special meaning. As with tarot cards, the symbolism needs to be understood. It is less easy to use inspiration with the runes than the Tarot and I don't recommend them for people without a good memory.

Tea leaf and coffee reading

Reading the tea leaves left in a cup after a person has drunk from it is called tassology. Here you are using psychometry as you can feel the energy of the person from the cup. Also, the tea, coffee or other residue left in the cup or glass can form patterns. One pattern may look like a bear, which could be a sign for you to tell the person that they need to embrace their own strength.

It is said that the residue by the handle is what is coming to you, while that which is furthest from the handle is leaving your life, or is in the past. The trick is not to try too hard – just let your mind drift.

Exercise: Tea leaf reading

Make a pot of tea using loose tea leaves. Pour the tea into a cup (don't use a tea strainer) and drink the tea. When you are down to the dregs, swirl the cup around three times in an anti-clockwise direction. Then, using your left hand, turn the cup upside-down on a saucer. Turn it once anti-clockwise and then turn the cup back upright. Meditate on the patterns left by the tea leaves and let images develop in your mind without forcing them. The important thing is the inspiration from the pattern and not the movement of the cup, that's just nice ceremony!

Graphology

This is the art of understanding a person from their handwriting. Each swirl and loop is said to carry significance, as well as the slant of the writing, the size of the margins, the spaces between letters and lines, and the thickness and size of the strokes. Most of this is a matter of common sense, and some psychometry. In the same way that a practical woman might wear flat shoes, a confident person would have big bold letters in their signature.

Numerology

The vibration of a person's name brings into being their life's purpose. Like the day on which we were born, it's possible that the name we were given is no accident. In numerology there is much the same significance in the numbers of a person's name and date of birth.

Exercise: Numerology

To find your birth number, first add up your birth date numbers (for example, 12 January 1976 = 1 + 2 + 1 + 1 + 9 + 7 + 6 = 27), then add the resulting numbers together (2 + 7 = 9).

The basic significance of the primary numbers is as follows:

ONE: Powerful, unique, confident, logical, independent, leadership.
TWO: Inner beauty, sensitivity, balance and harmony.
THREE: Healing, teaching, growth, creative power, enthusiastic.
FOUR: Practical, wise, dependable.
FIVE: Changeability, variety and freedom of expression.
SIX: Balance through conflict, nurturing, improving.
SEVEN: Creative and independent, self-expression, attention to detail.
EIGHT: Prosperity, stability and continuity of purpose.
NINE: Spiritually strong, likes to travel and learn, perfectionist and likes to help others.

Exercise: Reading from names

Ask the client to write down the full name of someone they want information on. In the same way that you can read anything – tarot cards, tea leaves or even strawberries – allow the name to inspire you. A person's name brings into being their life's purpose. So what's in a name? Everything!

For example: Justin Oates.

You can see which parts of the name stand out, the JUST in Justin, or the IN part. What does that tell you? Just in time? Just in case?

Or what if the 'I' stands out? Is this person quite into themselves? You can see how this works with any name.

The pendulum

The pendulum has also been recognised throughout the ages as a tool of perception. Over the centuries midwives have dangled a wedding ring on the end of a piece of thread over an expectant mother to determine the sex of the child. The pendulum can be any weighted object on a thread, chain or string.

When I first started using the pendulum, I asked questions I knew the answer to, such as am I wearing pink knickers. I then wanted to know where the answers were coming from. After asking if it was me, my higher self or my spirit guide, and finding that all the answers were coming up no, I asked if it was God. The pendulum then went to yes! Oops, sorry I asked about knickers!

Exercise: Using the pendulum

Taking the string of the pendulum in a relaxed grasp between the thumb and forefinger of the hand you normally write with, place your other hand in a position underneath.

Keep the arm holding the pendulum close to your body to avoid causing swinging from movement in the arm.

Firstly, you need to determine how the pendulum will move for the answers yes and no.

Ask the pendulum to show you how to recognise the answer yes. The movement it makes will be how you recognise the answer yes to your questions. It could be a swing to the right, to the left, clockwise, anti-clockwise or up and down.

Now repeat the exercise asking for the movement to show you the answer no.

Then ask if the pendulum is willing to work with you. If the answer is no, try again later. If yes, ask a few questions, where you will know the answers, and see what the responses are. Once you have established that you are connecting with the pendulum satisfactorily, you can move on to questions that you don't know the answer to.

Exercise: Answering questions

Hold the pendulum in the manner described above, state the topic of your question and ask 'Can I ask about this?' If you receive a yes, go ahead with your question. If not, choose another question.

Ask your question and, if it helps, say the question out loud.

The pendulum may start to move slowly or quickly, but give it time to swing into a definite position so that it is clear whether the answer is yes or no. Half signals such as a vague movement clockwise could indicate that you need to ask your question again more clearly. Try again.

When you have received your reply, be sure to say thank you.

Scrying

Scrying is most commonly known as crystal ball gazing, and has been used for many years as a focus for clairvoyant sight. When your physical sight is focused on a non-stimulating object your clairvoyant sight opens up, allowing you to access your third eye chakra. A crystal ball is used for the energy of the crystal, but anything can be used. Focusing on any object allows the mind to become like a canvas for any psychic impressions you may receive.

Exercise: Scrying

Use a bowl of water and a wax candle. Pour the hot wax into the water to form patterns. These patterns might be in the shape of something. See what meanings these shapes may have for you. Do they relate to your past and possibly a lesson you haven't learnt? Or is it a symbol? For example, a bear might mean you need to embrace your inner strength.

The competition between psychics

At a psychic fair, I witnessed one psychic sweeping their arm across a table another psychic had set up, sending tarot cards and crystal balls flying across the room. This was because that psychic had taken the table that the other psychic had 'always had', the one by the door. I have found among psychics a level of professional jealousy that I never encountered even in my years working with actors.

Being psychic doesn't make you spiritual, although I strongly think it should, and my only explanation for this attitude is one that I have seen at drama school. At secondary school, there is always one especially talented person at drama, the one that always gets the lead in the school play. That person then goes to drama school and their amazing talent becomes normal when compared to the talents of the other students.

Like it or not, a psychic likes to have skills that others don't have. In the ego, most people like to be special and work hard at being the best at something, to have an amazing skill. When you get a group of psychics together it's a case of fight for your special ability or face becoming normal! I have even seen psychic development tutors do this with talented students, knocking them down so they don't have the competition.

All I can say (to stop this ever becoming you) is, 'What is yours will not pass you by.' We are all one, there is no separation. As Jesus said, 'What I can do you can also do and greater.' These gifts are accessible to all, not just the few. But lastly, you are only as good as your last reading. Some days you will be excellent, some days you will be average. It's better to stay humble and then you never have to fall from the dizzying heights of the ego.

Setting up

Here are a few practical tips to help you on your way to setting up a practice.

Bookshops, Colleges and Institutes: Every place you will work is likely to charge a different split. Often the split is 50/50. Don't accept any split less in your favour, unless it's a phone reading set up.

The plus side of working for someone else is they will do the marketing for you. However, I strongly recommend you have your own fliers printed – plain black and white with your photo on it will do. Remember that the more upmarket you go with fliers, the more people will think you are a fake or that you are very expensive. Odd but true! It would normally be a mark of professionalism.

Also, keep a file of all of your letters of recommendation and thanks. This is a good thing to keep around for people to see, especially if there is anything about you in the media. Whenever you give a tape, put your card in the case or make your own tape case covers (they are really easy and cheap to make). This ensures that if a person keeps the tape, which they will if it was a good reading, they will also have your details so that they can come and see you again or recommend you to someone else.

From home

At home you are not paying for room hire, so you can charge less than the shops in town. Also, if you don't live in the centre of town, a money incentive is a good idea, to encourage people to travel that bit further. In my experience, people don't like to travel. I have an office in Piccadilly and the College of Psychic Studies in South Kensington, both on the Piccadilly line with only a few stops between them. However, people still will wait an extra week to see me at Piccadilly as they say they don't want to go all the way out to South Kensington. That's living in London for you!

Room rents

There are many great office spaces you can rent, and you could even go in with other psychics and healers, especially as I doubt you would need the room every day, which could be a heavy financial commitment. I rent a room for one day a week, paying on a monthly basis; even if I do not use the room one week, I still have to pay. Therefore, make sure you have the clients already in place. It is very important to have a space with a waiting area and even having a receptionist (which often comes with the office space). The reason for this is because you can't greet your client while you are in a reading with someone else, and if the client is early then it can mess up the flow of the reading. It is vastly preferable to have someone who can greet the client and show them where to wait, while letting you know that they have arrived.

Make sure that every venue has a toilet. This might sound unimportant, but if your client has been crying they will want to clean up. Also, if a client needs the loo during a reading, they won't be able to concentrate on you.

Recording

Recording on to a tape is the easiest way to record sessions, and you can still buy cheap tapes if you want to give clients copies of the reading. But remember that times are changing and many people don't have tape players any more. There are ways of recording onto a disc via a computer, but I find that this method tends to take up too much time. Soon we will have the technology to record directly onto a disc. That's not a future prediction, just a guess.

In the space

* Have water for yourself and the client.
* Tissues, but not obviously in sight as this can make a client feel like they are coming for a counselling session. They are, of course, but we don't want to give them the idea that we expect them to cry.
* Table and two chairs.
* If you use any tools, such as Tarot cards, place them on a cloth on the table. It also helps to spread the cards out across the table if you don't cut the pack.
* A lit candle (as long as it complies with the fire regulations of the building). Don't use any scent or incense, not everyone likes it.
* Tape recorder and tapes, spare batteries if needed.
* Something for you to do in case of a no show. Best not to get bored, it lowers your energy.
* Food to nibble on – carrots are great.

* Soft lighting, a table lamp is very good.

Breaks between readings

Depending on how deeply in vibration you work, I would say four to five readings per day is enough, especially if you do this every day. Most people can make evening and weekend appointments, but remember, you also need to have time for yourself and a life of your own. I currently only have two evenings a week free, which isn't such a problem for me as I am used to working evenings because of my previous career in the theatre – but in the theatre I had days off, a luxury I don't get much now. Take a 15-minute break in-between each client. All this makes a six-hour day or seven if you include a lunch break. Whilst not matching with the normal eight hour office day, is in fact normal for a counselling profession.

Testimonials and work curriculum-vita

It is hard to have a work résumé, but keep a list of dates and periods of work in different shops or at different events. It's a good idea to get a reference from the shop manager.

Also, keep a smart folder or file for any newspaper reviews or letters of thanks. If any testimonials come to you as e-mails, print them out and store them in your folder, something which has been very handy for me in the past. If you want to work at psychic fairs or any venue where people haven't come across you via word of mouth, this folder is a handy portable testimonial to have. Remember to hide all of the client addresses and contact details, as well as any personal information. If possible, it is also a good idea to get the clients' permission to show their letters; you'll find that happy customers will be keen to help let other people know about you.

Have a good website and keep it updated as much as you can because people often repeat visit to see what you are up to. However, bear in mind that people who are sceptical, and would like to sabotage you, can also keep an eye on your website.

Getting into the media

To make a living as a psychic, you need to spread the word and have good reviews in the media. Most people don't like to sell themselves because they think that it can be seen as un-spiritual. From my own experience, a reporter once came to me for a reading with the intention of writing an exposé called 'Clairvoyant or Con.' I, of course, wasn't seen as a con, and I wasn't able to cope with the amount of readings the article generated.

Do:

Most magazines and papers need an idea for a story. Think of it as doing them a favour, but you must come up with an idea for an article. Plan three months in advance of events happening: say, for example, you want to write about psychic love for February 14, then send the proposal in November.

Don't:

Contact the editor and say 'Hi, I'm a psychic and I would like to be featured.' Without an idea for an article, they won't be interested.

Do:

Research your magazines. I once did a prediction for *Loaded* magazine about football in my mind. It was only for fun and I explained you can't predict the future. Of course, they didn't print anything I said that really meant anything and even changed some of my answers; they even put me in a Mystic Meg wig! The end result was that I gave the sceptics a field day, as they thought I was being serious. However, a man did win £500 from placing a bet on the description I gave of the highest goal scorer. Think before you act – is it publicity you want or credibility?

Do:

Offer free readings to journalists. Be warned, they are some of the hardest people to read for as they are often thinking of the next question to ask you, and they find metaphors difficult to understand. They like facts and dates.

Do:

Look into the Ofcom (governing complaints body for all TV and radio programming) ruling when it comes to television or radio. If a station gets an Ofcom complaint because of something you said, you won't be used again. You can find the rules at: www.**ofcom**.org.uk

Don't:

Say yes to every TV show. But remember, recorded TV and radio programmes can be edited, whilst live shows can't. Live TV and radio shows are great as you can't be edited to look like a fool. However, you might not be able to tune in and could land flat on your face, so be aware of what you're saying at all times.

The first time you do anything in the media you will feel nervous. The best way to view it is as an enjoyable piece of light exploration. If you're having fun then you will come across as knowledgeable and confident. Never take yourself too seriously and try not to go down the road of fitting into the psychic stereotype, as you might find it hard to leave behind this image as you develop your work.

Do:

Keep contact details of all of the media people you work with. Update them on your work, even if it's a workshop or an event you know wouldn't make a story. It keeps you in their mind and you never know what they are working on that you could be involved with.

Don't:

Pay too much attention to others' comments on what they thought of you in the media. People do become jealous, and with the wonderful internet you can find reviews about yourself. It's sometimes a good idea to do a search of your own name, but make sure you have a thick enough skin before you do.

Please see the back of the book for a list of contacts in the media.

Handling readings

Let's take a moment just to think about what it is to give a reading. In short, someone is about to give your words a lot of weight in their life. Your words are about to influence a person with a more powerful impact than an advert for a soft drink. The flip side of this is that you could turn out to be a big disappointment for someone who has come to you for help. Even worse, you could say something that could damage a person.

I don't think people really realise the pressure of giving a reading. The psychic is opening themself up to picking up the other person's energy, including the person's emotions. It's not often a client will come to see you when they are happy. You are vulnerable to your client as much as they are vulnerable to you, and psychic protection as detailed in part two is very important.

When I first started as a professional psychic, I worked in a room in a theatre and all of the appointments were booked by me, with the clients finding me through word of mouth or from picking up a flier in the esoteric shops around London. When I finally took a job at one of the esoteric shops, I found myself sitting in a damp basement, in a small room the size of a toilet. I would take with me books to read and my laptop so that I could write articles. Most days I only would only get to see three clients, despite sitting there from 12.00pm until 7.00pm, just in case someone came in. The funny thing is, when I heard someone from the shop make their way down the stairs, my blood would run cold. The cheery shop assistant's voice would say 'Becky, you're wanted.' I would pause for a moment, then make my way upstairs to greet the client and bring them down into the little room with the door that didn't shut properly. (The only other option to this room was the shop window!)

In the moment before going upstairs, I would have the 'can I do this' conversation with myself, asking spirit for guidance and checking I was open and protected. Normally, my readings went well and I have been lucky enough to meet some amazing people.

Now that I am in my own office, when reception calls through and lets me know my client has arrived, I still get the same old feelings. Less intense, but still the wish to do the best job I can, to change someone's life for the better. When you know you have achieved this, there is nothing like it. I think this is the reason why readings are addictive, the very first buzz being when someone's eyes become wide, and you can see for yourself the change that your reading has made in that person. The person who came to see you was hopeless and afraid, now they are ready to take on the world. As psychics, we seek to do this as much as possible, but it's never enough.

Views on readings

A psychic and their client will have two different view points about what makes a good and a bad reading. It's worth thinking through what you feel makes a good reading, so that you have a type of checklist to refer to. You can't really rely on the client simply looking happy, like a hairdresser would, because you may start to find that when they are able to take a long hard look at themselves, they don't look happy, and you might think the reading is not a success!

What makes a good reading?

Client: Coming out with the answers you were looking for.

Being made to feel better.

Psychic: Picking up on undeniable jaw-dropping facts you couldn't have known.

Making the client feel better and giving them a new focus so that they can lead a more empowered life.

What makes a bad reading?

Client: Psychic not tuning in.

Psychic: Client being difficult or asking the same questions over and over even though you have explained the answer in many different ways.

When readings don't work!

Sometimes a reading doesn't work, and for some people it never works. What's the problem? The simple answer is energy! A client may come for a reading and not want it to work. That might sound odd, after all why would they pay the money? But sometimes it's worth the money to add to a list of problems: 'I even went to a psychic and they couldn't help me!'

I am normally well aware of when the energy between two people isn't going to be successful. You may spend some time trying to turn it round, and using humour is a good way of doing this, but stop the reading within 15 minutes if things haven't improved by then. Make sure that the client doesn't pay: it's worth saving your reputation.

If **you** are receiving a reading and the psychic hasn't tuned into you within 15 minutes, get up and leave the reading, without paying. I wish I had done that in the past, rather than put up with a disappointing session. When you are desperate for answers you will stay, hoping it will get better. It won't; if the psychic hasn't formed an understanding of you within 15 minutes then it's unlikely they will for the rest of the hour. It could be that the psychic isn't talented, or that the energy isn't right between you.

There can be many reasons for the energies 'not clicking' in a reading. It is, however, important to know that the client may not realise that you are not connected – they may just be thinking that you have some horrible information about them which you are not revealing! In all likelihood, the reason for the energy block could simply be a dislike of the client. It's a hard thing to have to tell someone, 'I can't work with you… because I don't like you.'

I have a three-smile rule – I smile at the door, when we sit, and when I start. If I have not had a smile back in that time, I don't begin the reading. It sounds hard, but when you are giving readings you are open and vulnerable. Don't risk your energy; if you don't feel right with someone, don't read.

Reasons for a reading not working

It is often tempting after a bad reading to blame yourself, thinking you are rubbish, especially if the client then believes you're a charlatan. Even the world's greatest psychics will find themselves struggling in some situations. It is hard to explain what is happening when a reading does not work, just as it is often difficult to explain in everyday terms what is happening when a reading does work, especially since each reading has a dynamic of its own and no two can be exactly alike. Broadly speaking though, a reading relies on the flow of energy between the psychic, the client and spirit. When there is a block in the flow of energy, the reading won't work. This energy block can either come from the psychic, the client or, occasionally, from spirit. It could be that the psychic is causing the block by their own life issues – we are, after all, only human. Or, the block may be from spirit who always works for your best interests and may not wish you to hear something until you are ready. More often, however, I have found that the block is coming from the client.

Blocking

This can happen because the client perhaps wants a reading but doesn't want to be a part of that reading. By not wanting to give anything away, they won't allow the reader to have an open flow of connection. Of course the client doesn't need to actually say very much. They could be behind a screen or 100 miles away on the end of a phone and say nothing, but by *wanting* the reading to be successful, there will be an open flow of connecting energy and it will work.

The client's spirit guide won't communicate information if the client is a private person. This also explains why when asked to look at a person on behalf of the client, say for example the client's father. You cannot see anything if the client's father is a private person, or would not go and see a psychic themselves. This gives people privacy from psychic spying, which we must respect.

You can also block by not wanting to hear something bad. I've been blocked from looking at someone's relationship because they didn't want bad news, whilst the rest of the reading was accurate.

A client sitting with arms folded and a demanding look on their face also doesn't help.

At the end of the day our job is to help people; to admit needing help is a hard thing to do. The most accurate readings are when someone really needs that help, and sometimes spirit surprises me with the level of detail and accuracy that I am given as a result of this call for help. When someone comes to see me out of curiosity, the information may come across as bland as there are no big earth-shattering pieces of information. But telling a client that everything is running to plan can be important as it may stop them from worrying.

Future predictions

People sometimes tell me that they went for a reading with another psychic and no future predictions came true, so they have come to see me instead. I don't believe in telling the future and make sure to I say before every reading: 'You're future isn't set in stone.' I can give the client the most likely outcome based on action, or lack of action, using the advice gained from spirit. Very few of us, myself included, have a full sense of the perspective of the present in our everyday lives due to the fact that we are learning. If we had all the answers what would be the point? A reading helps you *find* the answers but won't give them to you.

Imagination

The chalkboard that spirit uses to give us clairvoyant information is our imagination. The cinema screen that flashes up impressions during a reading is the same part of the mind that produces impressions when we are daydreaming. Sometimes imagination is stronger than psychic information, something that can happen to every psychic especially if the client asks you a question and your first response is to search your own mind for an answer. As psychics we have to give information without trying to interpret it, as our interpretation can be based on our own life experiences and not those of the client.

If a client tries to put pressure on the psychic by asking questions and demanding answers, the psychic will find it hard to respond. Psychics are people too, and under interrogation will respond like a person and clam up or not be able to focus.

Love

This may sound odd, but during a reading I truly love my client. It's the unconditional love of spirit; I'm energised by it and if that love isn't there, I won't read. However, that love can leave before the reading time is over and it is at this point that I know the advice is coming from me rather than spirit and I will say so. Spirit allows me to use my own skills of empowering and counselling; these are also vital for the reading. Like any story, a reading must have a beginning (who you are as a person, so I know I have connected with you), middle (all the reasons you have come to see me, without you having to ask me any questions) and an end (help and empowerment with all these issues).

It's hard to for me to remember anything I have said once the reading has ended, mainly because most of it is channelled.

Burn out

This is something we think will never happen to us, but it does happen to psychics all the time.

When I was developing as a medium, I really admired the American medium John Edward. I knew he was constantly booked up, yet in his books he talked about how much he loved watching TV. A thought crossed my mind, namely that if I had mediumship skills to his standard I would be doing sittings all the time, never stopping to watch TV. I now understand why that's simply not possible.

Psychic readings, and especially mediumship sittings, are draining. The work itself isn't what makes it so draining; it's everything that comes along with the work. If you don't look after yourself – eat well, exercise, sleep and give yourself time off – you can burn out. You may be too busy to notice that this is happening, so here are some clues:

A lack of focus in conversations, especially with friends.
Listen to your friends: people will start making comments about their worries for you.
Forgetting things, especially names.
Difficult sleep patterns: insomnia or waking up more tired.
Body not functioning well.
Not eating. Craving sugar and carbohydrates.
Finding loud noises disturbing.
Getting annoyed at small things.
When in meditation or falling asleep you see nasty little faces on the back of your eyelids.
Crying and being sensitive to anything and everything, including feeling paranoid.
No time for yourself.
Clients cancelling at the last minute or not getting any bookings. (This can be spirit's way of making you rest.)

Hassle

Sadly, this job, like any other, has its drawbacks. For example, the phone rings at all times of the night. This can be because the client wants you to realise how desperate they are, and often you will find there was no rush apart from a need for the client to control their own anxiety. Don't get sucked into losing the quality of your own life. If you do, you won't last as a psychic. You must have your own time over the need to help others. You can't do it 24 hours a day, but people will expect it as you are a spiritual helper.

The other expectation is that people expect you to do readings for free. As with most psychics, you have spent money on your training and, above all, spent time to get to the point you are at now, and it is only sensible that you try to cover these costs. However, I also believe that every psychic should work for a donation or for free whilst developing, and never charge for a bad reading.

The other day a woman sent me an e-mail (one of the many long e-mails I receive) filled with questions and requests for free advice. In reply I just answered her overall question, but I knew from experience that this could develop into an e-mail chat that I didn't have time for. For some psychics, it's a hobby, but I live and breathe the work, so, after answering the question for free, I then said any further questions must be asked by phone during a paid appointment. This was the reply:

> *'Many thanks for your prompt reply. It saddens me to see that you have such a great gift but are so very much money orientated. Anyway, thanks once again for your input to help me understand what may be happening. As you say you have a mountain of e-mails so I will let you get on in doing what you feel is important to you.'*

What is important to me is to have my time and my work respected. Others will judge you, but their judgement speaks more about them than you.

The most difficult things about the job:

* Phone calls on the mobile when people are trying to judge your spiritual nature while you are doing your shopping. (I know I shouldn't answer the phone!)

* People think you are constantly picking up information about them all the time.
* The expectation that all psychics do the same thing. Not all solicitors deal with property!
* Being seen as a fake.
* Other 'spiritual' people's judgements.

This might sound like a bit of a rant, but it's important if you come across these things to know that you are not the only one!

The best thing about the job is changing people's lives. I also love the e-mails of thanks, and seeing the realisation in people's eyes when something clicks for them. For me, it's the best job in the world.

A week in the life of a full-time psychic

If you are thinking of becoming a full-time psychic, you may be interested to know what an average week is like when working in this field. Here are some insights from three experienced psychics.

Becky Walsh

Monday:

Get up 8.00am. Have breakfast and walk the dog.

Leave for readings at the College of Psychic Studies 9.00am.

Arrive at 10.00am. Roughly 30 minutes meditation and room clearing.

Four clients. First client 10.30am, followed by 11.45am, 1.00pm and 2.15pm appointments. 15-minute break in-between clients to return phone calls and clear room and self for next client.

Finish at 3.15pm. Nip out for some lunch, and reply to e-mails in internet café. Back at college for 5.00pm to teach foundation group in psychic development. Intermediate group starts at 7.00pm.

Leave for home 8.30pm. Arrive home 9.30pm, short walk dog, check answer phone and reply e-mails.

Tuesday:

Get up 8.00am. Have breakfast and walk the dog.

Return yesterday's phone messages. Write whatever it is I'm working on (e.g. magazines, books and phone readings). Catch up on normal life.

Leave for college 5.00pm to teach short course. At 7.00pm advanced course in psychic development.

Wednesday:

Get up 8.00am. Have breakfast and walk the dog.

Leave for readings at the College of Psychic Studies 9.00am

Arrive at 10.00am. Return yesterday's phone messages. Roughly 30 minutes meditation and room clearing.

Three clients. First client 10.30am, followed by 11.45am and 1.00pm appointments. 15-minute break in-between clients to return phone calls and clear room and self for next client.

Finish at 2.00pm. Go to the gym, get some lunch and reply e-mails in internet café.

Back at college 4.45pm for three more clients: 5.00pm, 6.00pm and 7.00pm. Leave at 8.00pm. Arrive home 9.00pm, walk dog, check answer phone and reply e-mails.

Thursday:

Get up 8.00am. Have breakfast and walk the dog.

Return yesterday's phone messages.

Leave for office in Piccadilly 10.30am. Arrive 11.30am Roughly 30 minutes meditation and room clearing.

First client 12.00pm, followed by 1.00pm, 2.00pm, 3.00pm, 4.00pm, 5.00pm, and 6.00pm appointments. (All clients can have up to an hour but often a whole hour isn't needed. There are also more 'no shows' on a Thursday as people don't pay in advance as they do at the college. Not taking a break means I don't lose too much money on the no shows, but some days it doesn't pay off.)

Leave at 7.00pm. Arrive home 8.00pm, walk dog, check answer phone and reply e-mails.

Friday:
Anything that needs doing: planning live radio shows, e-mails, calling people back, articles, cleaning, phone readings, shopping and meeting friends.

Leave at 6.30pm for the LBC 97.3 studio for the radio show. Home 2.00am.

Saturday:
Phone readings, planning college lessons, catching up on all work, and getting over last night's show.

Sunday:
Have a life.

Emails: 20 per day approx, not including radio show mail.
Phone calls: Home 5; Mobile 5 per day approx.

July 2006.

Inbaal

Monday
Woke up early knowing I had eight e-mail readings waiting on my hard drive, as well as a feature to write for the coming issue of the Japanese ELLE girl. I made a start on the readings, which were a bit slow going, but the feature for ELLE was written in 13 minutes while having my lunch.

A doctor's appointment at 5.00pm broke up the day nicely and allowed me a bit of fresh air. My back and neck have been suffering from too many hours on the phone giving readings, and the doctor referred me to an osteopath.

At 8.00pm went in to do a shift on the Psychic Interactive Channel, which finished at 2.00am.

This was a hard day.

Tuesday

Woke up at my boyfriend's and figured I'd be bored with a whole day off, so did all his ironing and washing up. Staggered home in the afternoon to lie in front of the telly all day.

This was an easy day.

Wednesday

Early shift on Psychic Interactive, and not allowed to be late any more (have been late for kindergarten, school and jobs every day of my life) so arrived 15 minutes before 8.30am, start time. Afterwards rushed home for a phone reading. Someone bought his sister a reading for her birthday, which was nice to do. Went to the cinema in the evening. the evil character.

This was a tiring, long day.

Thursday

15 e-mail readings. Ignored my cousin who tried to ring me to meet up all day. She'll be in London again in a couple of years' time. This day was hard on my family.

Friday

Spent three hours cleaning my tiny studio from top to bottom and still not perfect (I'm trying to sell it). A guy came to view it but didn't put in an offer. Two e-mail readings. Back to Psychic Interactive evening shift till 2am.

This day didn't feel like a Friday.

Saturday

Woke up, packed and made my way to Roehampton, where a couple wanted me to bless their baby. It was lovely to name her and bless her in the names of the elements, the ancient ones and the Lord and Lady. The family was super-nice to me. They might take me if my real family rejects me.

A really fun day.

Sunday

Went for a very long walk by the river, then back into the TV studio until 2.00am. I worked with two of my favourite psychics there, and in the absence of a presenter we presented the show ourselves. It was a brilliant challenge and the producer was particularly complimentary.

This was a fulfilling day.

http://www.inbaal.com

Michael Korel

My psychic work is channelled, if you'll excuse the pun, into banks of time. It used to be that I was always open but that turned into quite a strain, so now I usually only do readings on Mondays, Wednesdays and Fridays – of course it has to be flexible but I have to physically and spiritually look after myself and the interests of my clients. I discovered when I started doing this as a living that you can work too much.

Monday is private client day. I am really selective as I simply don't want to take on more clients than I can give my utmost to. People put a lot of faith in us and we owe it to them to be at our best when they come to see us.

Wednesday and **Friday** are the days that I do my nightclub work. This wasn't something I fell into, rather I picked the environment because I wanted to give people who never have or would never think of going to see a psychic the opportunity to do so. It's hard and it's loud so I need to protect myself physically and psychically. I do vocal warm-ups to make sure that I don't lose my voice, and I do a protection ritual for myself and the club to keep out harmful spirits. I do a lot of parties and launches, but I am resident at Chinawhite and I was there before it opened and worked (alongside a feng shui consultant) to create a conducive space for my work in a place that wouldn't necessarily be conducive. But if you're working in an unfamiliar space then having candles or crystals or whatever makes you feel comfortable is always worthwhile.

The other bit is writing and broadcasting. I used to write several columns a week for magazines and websites and a weekly radio show (this was music and chat-based with a psychic segment rather than a psychic show like Becky's!). I now write for newspapers and guest on radio shows but the process of preparation is still the same, and this goes for all aspects of my work, I start every day with a two part meditation. A chakra opening meditation followed by an automatic response writing practice. This combination encompasses so many parts of what I do and what I enjoy and sets me up for whatever is going to come my way. There's always something to distract you from doing these rituals and I have shortened versions of both, but we should never cut them out entirely, trust me on that. It's the first step to becoming complacent and it's important work that we're doing.

I have two pieces of advice for anyone following a psychic path:

1) being psychic is a gift and gifts should be shared. That doesn't mean that you shouldn't be allowed to make a living doing it but when it becomes just a job then it inevitably loses something.

2) Take your work but not yourself seriously.

Running circle groups and workshops

It was in the séance room that the 'circle group' was first formed. Sitting in a circle is used as a way to develop mediumship because spirit needs the energy of the living to be able to move or communicate in this physical dimension, and by sitting in a circle no one person is drained of energy more than any other. This gives support to the medium and developing mediums.

In the same way that spirit can use the energy of others, the living can also use the energy of people. Therefore, by sitting in a circle it also means that the perhaps more draining or dense vibrations of one person are diluted around the group. Likewise, it also allows more positive energy to be sent around the circle.

The round table plays its part in giving us insight into the mind of King Arthur; the idea is not to have one person at the head of a table or anyone above another. A group that has sat together for a long time may become a closed circle, with no one else joining it, which can be useful for developing mediumship, but can have the opposite effect for psychic development. If you know the lives of everyone in the group, how can you prove you are picking up information on a psychic level?

It is a very good idea, even for the most experienced psychic medium, to keep a development circle. Even if you are the teacher of that group, you learn just as much from the group at times as you would if you were a student.

Getting a group started

Most people run circles from their home, which means that no room hire fee is incurred. However, pets and children can be unpredictable, so you must make sure you have a room where you won't be disturbed. You also need to make sure you have enough chairs and that they will fit in a circle around the table.

There should be a strong discipline regarding when people arrive and leave, so that no one is late and no one outstays their welcome with the host. Groups may move around to others' homes within the group, but if there is too much change, it can make it harder to raise the vibration of the group; bear in mind that a room holds the energy from the meetings that have taken place previously.

It is possible to hire a room, but remember the whole group will have to share the cost, regardless of whether members are able to attend or not. Otherwise you could find yourself paying for the whole room yourself because something great is on TV!

To find members of the group, try placing an ad in a newspaper such as Psychic News. You could also put up a flyer in an esoteric shop near you. You will be amazed at how many people will respond, especially if it's free. I am always being asked if I run a circle group.

Be aware that some people will join just to get readings and not wish to develop their own skills. It's harsh, but these people don't belong in the group. Always interview your group members to make sure the group dynamic is right. One difficult group member can result in you losing your group.

If you do find a group member with energy that is too strong for the group, try the following as it really helps on workshops or in a situation where you can't ask the person to leave the group.

Imagine a giant jam jar being placed over the group member you are having a situation with. This will contain the negative energy coming towards you or the group. Then, picture the person the way they would have looked when they were a child. See them now to be that child, unaware of the effect they are having on you and on the group, and visualise talking to them in that state. Tell them of the problem this is causing you, and reassure them that you will do everything in your power to understand them and to resolve this situation. Forgive the child-version of your group member, knowing it is really yourself you are forgiving.

Circle code of conduct

This will be personal to every group. However, there are a few ways in which to protect a group from some normal pitfalls that may occur. Most of these pitfalls are based on human nature rather than anything paranormal.

Try and insist that everyone make every meeting as this helps with the group dynamics and the vibration for development. If anyone isn't attending, they should send a message of apology. It isn't always possible to make every meeting, but if you as an individual take it seriously, then the whole group will do the same. When being told that someone can't make a meeting, never say, 'That's OK, don't worry.' Just tell them that you look forward to seeing them next time. There is little point in making a big statement at the beginning of a group about attendance, only to later say it doesn't matter!

At the beginning of the session

Bless the room with positive energy. The wording of this is up to you, but the idea is to bring a sense of harmony and positive energy to the space. Many places have more than one purpose; any energy that has been in the space may not hold the lightest of vibrations you need to be able to work. Using every member of the group, ask them to bring in that light and that harmony. In doing so they are also letting go of the journey they have taken to get to you, and bringing themselves into alignment with light and harmony. Asking people to release anything negative often makes them think of the negative thing they are releasing, which then brings it into the circle. I remember once being asked to let go of the journey I had taken to get to a meeting; I was then brought back to the annoying part of the journey and became frustrated about it all over again, which certainly didn't bring light and harmony to the occasion.

Once the room has a harmony and a focus, so does the circle group. Bring in also all of the people who are not in the circle who couldn't make it that week. Honour those people, wishing them well and ask that they receive the knowledge they would have gained in some other way. Bringing those people into the group shows there is still no separation between them and us, and also helps stop people talking behind backs of others.

Ask for spirit guides of those in the group to be present, and work for the greatest good. If the group is a mediumship development group, also ask for the loved ones of those present who reside in the spirit world to step forward with positive intent to help those developing.

The wording of this could be:

We bless this space in love, friendship and light. We ask spirit to join with us in bringing harmony into the space and into the hearts of every member of this circle. We also send out love to those who were unable to join us this week; we send out that the wisdom and knowledge brought forward into today's meeting find them in another way, and ask for our spirit guides and loved ones to be present and help us with our positive endeavours to further our development. So be it.

Then have a few moments silence before starting the group.

Latecomers

Anyone running late must let the group leader know, so that the room blessing can be done after their arrival. Anyone arriving after the blessing may not be admitted, depending on the group leader. This may seem hard, but in today's world of mobile phones, sending a message isn't difficult.

A one-day workshop

A one-day workshop can be a great way to start teaching. I started by hiring a room and inviting people I was giving readings to, as well as making a few flyers and placing them in esoteric shops. You can also make a circle group from the people who want to continue after the workshop.

A one-day psychic development workshop could include:

Opening and closing chakras and working with energy
Grounding and protection in everyday life
Reading tools, such as psychometry and Tarot
Inspirational speaking

How to tell the difference between your imagination and information
Giving a clear reading
Sensing colour

A workshop on mediumship might include:

Opening and closing chakras and working with energy
How to tell the difference between communication and imagination
Psychic protection and safe practice
Meeting your sprit guide
Working on platform
Getting validation from spirit
Sitting in the power
Meditation

Development games and workshop tools

To sit in a circle, bring messages and give readings to the members of the group is an enjoyable process. However, it is variation that keeps people coming back every week; after all, they won't want to miss anything. Here are some ideas that might inspire some of your own members when running a group. They are written from the perspective of a teacher to a student, that way you can read them out or use them as handouts. They are a mix of my own concepts and ones I have picked up over the years.

Exercise: Experience Chi energy

This Chi energy is available to us all at all times; it is said that you can live for a short time without food or water, but you can't live one second without Chi. In order to get a real experience of this energy, to really *feel* it, you can do this on a personal level with a group, with each member experiencing their own Chi, or with the Chi of the group as a whole.

Spend a moment focussing on breathing, then rub your hands together vigorously for a few seconds until you feel heat developing between the palms. Hold your hands twelve inches apart from each other. A tingling sensation in the palms and on your fingers will be felt. Next, move your hands back and forth to feel the energy. This is Chi. Now slightly curve your fingers as if you were holding a ball. Send through intention of your love and your power into that space between your hands. Wait for a little time for the energy to build up. Then slowly try and close your hands together. You will feel some resistance in the gap, as if you are holding a spongy rubber ball. This is your Chi, your life force, and hopefully you will have just demonstrated two things to the group; firstly, that Chi is real and can be felt, and secondly, that it responds to thought and intention, and can be manipulated. This also applies to any form of vibration.

Exercise: Viewing the Aura.

Place your hand on a sheet of white paper. Look at your hand but relax your eyes and allow them to lose focus. Around your hand you will start to see colour and a white edging. If you move your hand off the paper quickly, you might also see the trace of the aura left behind on the paper.

Exercise: Psychometry and the chair

Try sitting in a chair and feel your own energy in that chair, noticing what you feel like in that chair, how your body feels.

Then sit in someone else's chair – this can be fun to do on the bus or on a train. But try and choose a happy looking person as you don't want to take on board someone else's distressing energy.

See if you feel any different. Is there any information you get about this person? Any aches and pains you didn't have before? How tall do you feel? What's your body size? Any information you get can be psychic information and it may be worth trying this with someone you can talk to afterwards to fact-check the information that you are getting. You might be amazed by how accurate the information is that you pick up. This can also be a very useful exercise to see if the person you fancy is as nice as you thought they were by sitting in their chair!

Group meditations

A guided meditation is a great way to start a class. Here is a meditation idea set out for that purpose:

Meditation to meet your higher self

Focus your attention on your breathing.

Breathe in positive signs through the right nostril and breathe out negative signs through the left.

Allow the positive breath to fill you up until the negative breath going out becomes less and less negative and more positive; continue until you are only breathing out positive breath. Keep breathing out the positive breath until the whole room is full of positive energy.

Open the chakras.

Focus on the black of the back of your eyelids. See the black becoming further and further away from you, until it becomes the black of a pure night sky.

As you look you see stars start to form. They are twinkling in the dark sky.

As you look the stars start to move together and spell out your name.

Enjoy looking at your name spelt out in brilliant stars for the whole world to see how brilliant you are.

As you look you feel yourself becoming lighter.

You become lighter and lighter as if you weigh nothing at all.

You become so light that you are light itself and you find yourself floating upwards to join the stars.

Higher and higher you fly towards your name, until your name just turns back into hundreds of stars. Choose a star and fly towards it.

As you get closer you see the star is earth,

But it's not our earth.

Flying further you see your country, but it's not your country.

You see your town, but it's not your town.

You see your home, but it's not your home.

You find yourself outside your own front door, but it's not your front door.

Behind the door is you, but it's not you.

This is your higher self, the God that is inside you.

The door is opened and you see your higher self for the first time.

What do you look like?

You are taken to the most comfortable room in the house.

You can now sit and talk.

Is there something that your higher self wants to say to you?

Is there something that you would like to ask?

Your higher self would like you to meet someone.

Another door is opened in your home, but it leads to a different place.

This room is full of light and rainbows.

In front of you is your spirit guide.

What does it look like?

Your guide has something to say to you.

Now you, your higher self, and your spirit guide get the chance to talk.

Remember you can ask any questions, and if it is the right time, they will help you find the answers.

Your guide wants to give you healing, and you can feel the touch of their hands on your shoulders.

You can enjoy this feeling of their love for you and this healing energy.

It's almost time to come back now, so ask your guide and your higher self to lift from you any burden you have been holding on to that doesn't suit you, and transform it to positive learning energy.

Your spirit guide gives you a word to bring back with you.

Remember that word.

As you go to the door, your power animal is there to greet you.

See this animal now.

What animal is it?

It is there to guide you and give you a safe trip home.

You feel yourself becoming light again and flying back towards earth.

As you enter the earth's atmosphere you are greeted with many colours:

first white,

then violet,

then blue,

then green,

then yellow,

then orange,

then red.

As you sit, the red energy around you fades, and you feel your roots are back in place, linking you back to the earth.

Your power animal has gone back to a silent realm, but is always there if you need protection.

Bring your attention back to sitting in the room, back to the present, and open your eyes.

PART FIVE

RELATIONSHIPS

The majority of a psychic's work is related to relationships. It's easy to understand why, as relationships are the one thing in life we cannot control.

If we need more money or a new home, we find a way to change our circumstances to get what we need. In life, for most situations we can rely purely upon ourselves to do what we need, or pay someone else to help us. We even have some control over our health by watching what we eat, or by wearing sun cream. Whatever it is, we have some kind of input that can give us the outcome we desire. The one thing we cannot control, and neither should we, is another's free will.

But the fact is we need people and cannot live without them. Relationships affect everything we do and sometimes we need help dealing with them. Typically, someone will come to see a psychic to find out how another person feels about them, or how to unblock being single and find a relationship, or to see if a certain person is 'the one' – questions most of us have asked at one time or another. This chapter is to help you find the answers to these questions. It is also full of empowerment tools you can use for yourself, and to teach others.

Born into a relationship

We are all born into someone else's relationship. This is the starting point of all of our options in life as well as our perception of people and relationships; usually we see parents as being the guiding force. A person's personality is fully formed by the age of five, meaning that most of the things that happen before that time have great meaning for our future personality traits. The only problem is we can't always remember much of what happened before we were five. A child who sees their parent's lives as a disaster might look and think, 'Who would want to be a grown-up?' They may then go on to make a subconscious decision not to become a grown-up or commit to a relationship, as that's what grown-ups do and it makes them unhappy. This is the beginning of what people describe as the Peter Pan syndrome. There are many other decisions we make in childhood consciously or unconsciously.

Case study: The nanny

Neil was 18 months old he had his mum to himself. Then, when his mum gave birth to his brother, she went out to work and Neil and his brother had a nanny. This nanny was blonde; she got pregnant and left the job as she was about to give birth. The same thing happened with another five blonde nannies. Finally, a brown-haired nanny came, didn't get pregnant and stayed with Neil and his brother for many years.

Neil doesn't want children, hates the sight of pregnant women and has never dated a blonde!

Blocking the vulnerable role

The women's movement is a wonderful thing. However, both women and men are now struggling to find their feet in the world of sexual equality, which itself is also trying to find its feet. Women, although no longer as dependent on men, still hold tightly to the fear of dependency and worry about being vulnerable in some way. Being open in a relationship is about being vulnerable. The biological role of a man is to protect. We are moving away from our natural biological make-up. Yet we wonder why many women in their thirties are not able to find a father for the children they so desperately want. Like it or not, as a woman, to have children you will become vulnerable to the income and the care of your partner. If you are sending out a vibration that says you don't want to be dependent upon a man, you will also block the man who would like to take care of a family.

Women make that internal promise not to be vulnerable, but if they are not careful they cut out the option to have a relationship at all as the energy colour on their auric field becomes full of self-protection. As a provider, a man feels he needs to protect; he will reject a woman who is so strong that she has no need of him, and will look for a woman who does need him. It's not a conscious thing, but the message is clear in the energy field and the vibration that women send out.

We can change what our energy field is giving out by the way we think. The mind is very powerful and our positive intent can make a big difference. Many people have found this to work in the form of affirmations. It's as easy as making a decision or a choice, for if you can choose what you want, you can draw it to you. Every thought is creative; you create your life by your thoughts. This is known as the law of attraction. So if you are thinking all men are bastards, then bastards you shall meet.

The right attraction

We often look for people who are like us, but the most successful relationship can be with a person whose characteristics we need. For example, if you are a pushover it would be great to be with someone who is stubborn as they will, in turn, make you stronger. Being with someone who has something you lack can empower you to change, to fill in that gap. This makes the two of you like the ying and yang combination, one being white with a touch of black, and one being black with a touch of white. The perfect match.

Relationship of the highest intention

We create our frustrations through the influences of the outside world. The train was late, so I'm frustrated even though it hasn't made me late. Or, I haven't eaten properly so I'm crabby, and my boyfriend didn't react in the way I wanted to my new dress, so I'm even more annoyed.

There is so much frustration with how we expect the world to be and how we think it should serve us that little time is taken in looking at how we serve the world. So much of what annoys us is in our own control but we choose not to take the self-discipline required to fix it, or to think about our feelings in relation to the bigger picture. We should be thinking, ‘Just how important is this really, or am I making a drama because I feel better in the ‘poor me’ state?’ It truly isn’t always possible to work from our highest intention, but if we aim to we will be closer than we think.

What would our highest intention say to our lover? ‘I want for you, what you want for yourself.’ This is very easy to say, but not that easy to do. In saying this it doesn’t mean that you can stay in a relationship with someone who hurts you, just because if they want it then that’s what you have to want: some behaviour is simply unacceptable. Many of us start a relationship for a simple reason: ‘What can I get out of this person that will improve my life?’ Rarely do we think, ‘What can I add to this person’s life?’

It’s hard to draw a picture of how we want to be or who we want to be in our next or current relationship, because the chances are we don’t know what we are looking for. I can’t think of a single relationship where I have been who I truly want to be, i.e. my highest self. Most of us spend our time in the lower three chakras dealing with our fear issues. Even the emotion of falling in love, the ‘will he call me?’ phase, the excitement of open possibilities that are there to be discovered, is another form of anxiety. So what I’m saying is the largest emotion when falling in love is anxiety with a hint of joy. We start our communication in fear, ‘What can I have?’, and if we aren’t aware, it stays that way. The honest truth is that we are selfish beings and most of our motivation is for the self. If we don’t get what we want out of the relationship, we then leave that relationship and see it as no good. Once we become honest, we are dealing with our higher self, which brings with it unconditional love, as that is the love without fear. The only problem is we can’t unconditionally love others because to survive in everyday life we have to put ourselves first most of the time.

If we expand that further, for instance if we share our feelings of love with our lover, but never look to them to reduce those less-favoured feelings such as anxiety, we might find that it solves some problems in relationships. If I feel I'm fat, no amount of hearing my partner tell me I'm not will change how I feel, so why go on and on about it?

Making an investment of love

Many people judge their relationship by what they have put into it, using their investment as a measurement of what they should get out of it. When we meet someone who needs our help, we give them whatever it is that they need. And like a bird with a broken wing, when one day that wing becomes fixed, they fly away. Relationships are not a banking investment. What you put into a relationship has to be given with love, and let go of – you must not expect to earn 'interest' on the love you give. Otherwise, It will only make you bitter and angry if the relationship does not work out.

So how can you tell if a relationship has worked out? Well, we will only know that when we are in our eighties, or when our loved one has died. I believe that a relationship that is loving is always working. Inevitably love ebbs and flows like the tide, depending on how a couple relates. One day a person may be the apple of your eye, the next moment they may say or do something thoughtless that hurts. And now will you love this person any less? Love is made up of many things, and so is the way we measure how we love someone.

How to break obsessive love

Many clients will come to you with the question, 'Is he coming back to me?' Replying with a 'yes' may leave your client waiting for years, or you could also add to a dangerous obsession, dangerous because people can waste years. We all know that people find us most attractive when we are not needy, so finding a way to heal the need is the best thing you can do for this client, without answering the question.

When a person is obsessively in love with someone they can feel like they are going mad. These obsessions can last many years, sometimes without even seeing or hearing from the person they are hooked on.

The mind is a muscle and it can be trained as you can train any muscle, making it possible to control what you think. For example, when people say that they can't stop worrying, this isn't true. Worry is habit forming, just like smoking. Some people feel that they need to worry about something excessively in order to make it go right, like it's a superstition. Worry is thought. If we think positively, people call it daydreaming, but I know you can manifest a positive outcome by believing it to be positive. If you think negatively, that is considered preparation. But if that 'thinking on a negative' becomes a 'cycle of thought', which goes over and over and over in your mind, then that is what's known as worrying. That worry can have the same effect as a negative manifestation; we attract what we think about. The trick is to prepare for the worst whilst knowing you will have the best, and then let it go. It is the people who have a 'worry side' to their personality who tend to get obsessive about love. If you are like this yourself, or you see this in a client or friend, the way to break it is as follows:

1: Allow a thought of the person to come into your mind without beating yourself up over it. Let that thought be one thought and not a string of thoughts, all following on from that first thought.
2: Breathe deeply.
3: If the thought continues, replace it with another thought, which can be anything on a positive note.
4: Deny yourself the sexual fantasy of this person. If you really want to let them go, it has to be all aspects. Even sexual thoughts about a person create energy and cords.
5: Use cord cutting exercises in this book.
6: Keep your life busy with nice things to do and have in your life. Make time for friends, but don't use it as an opportunity to talk

about your obsession; it's most probably talked to death.

The love of your life

What makes someone the love of your life? Surely it is the person that you feel you have loved the most up to this point in life. But as we love in different ways, how can we compare one love with another?

You can only know the love of your life with hindsight, but hindsight is often seen through rose-tinted glasses. The love of your life is the one you felt the most emotion for, but that emotion might have been as painful as it was earth-shattering. For example, a well-known singer friend of mine once told me how she loved her husband deeply, but that the love of her life was a gangster she knew in her early twenties. He had made those years the most exciting and emotionally turbulent time of her life. However, the loving relationship she currently experiences with her husband gives her a much more fulfilling and contented life.

The right or wrong partner

I do not think there is such a thing as the wrong partner. People are put in your life for a reason, to teach you a lesson. How many times have you seen a pattern in people's relationships, the same things happening over and over again, perhaps even mimicking their parents' relationships? As the saying goes, the definition of stupidity is doing the same things and expecting different results. I believe there are always warning signs that a relationship is going wrong; we can still trust our sixth sense to see these signs, but the trick is to trust ourselves to act upon those instincts. The problem is that we often choose to ignore these signs, out of fear, and many of us hang on to a relationship even when we know it's doomed. It's only human.

The key to success is to attract a person who matches your personality. You need to find an aspect in the partner that you are lacking or holding back. I hate the thought of being bossy and controlling as I think that these traits are negative, so I hide those parts of my personality. As a result, I might find myself in a relationship with a controlling person.

Being controlling isn't a negative trait, it's how you use it. There are no negative personality traits, it's how we use them. If I employed a builder to build a wall, and I came home to find no wall and the builder having a cup of tea watching my TV, being controlling would be a skill I would need, otherwise I would be a walkover!

Have a look at your partner's qualities and see if there are qualities in you that he/she would benefit from, and vice versa. If there is an aspect of yourself you haven't come to terms with, then you may find that aspect in your partner. So, if you hide the insecure part of yourself, you may find yourself with insecure people.

If you are with someone who is abusing you, they have to be told that this isn't correct behaviour. Even the abuser is being abused if they are allowed to carry on in this way. If the abuser sees that the behaviour isn't acceptable, they will learn from it, perhaps making it possible for them to save themselves and possibly save the relationship.

The meeting of souls

I remember a client of mine saying she only wanted to be in a relationship with someone she had a past life connection with, which would block any new connections in this life time. I had to point out that she still had to make connections for the next lifetime. Two souls can choose to be linked together from one lifetime to the next, normally because they agree to learn lessons from each other in each lifetime. Meeting a soul mate has a similar feel to meeting a past life partner: the feeling that you have known them before.

Normally, soul mates meet in very odd circumstances, and they often wonder why they have not met before as they share the same interests, have been to the same places at the same time, have had the same friends for years, or even say the same words at the same time. They might even have had the same type of bad past experiences in their lives.

It is very exciting to meet someone like this. It really makes your heart flutter for suddenly you realise that you are not alone. All the things that you think about yourself as being daft or silly, somebody else shares this with you. In that moment, we feel less alone and the future looks bright. This, for me, is the right person for right now. As I say, there are no such things as coincidences. So when all these things are found in one person, sit up and listen!

A kindred spirit is like a soul mate as there is a sense of understanding and great warmth. But you are on the same learning level, not discovering more from each other, and this will make you feel as if something is missing in the relationship, even though it can go on for many years.

A past life love partner is different from a soul mate or kindred spirit. The same connections are there, but so much stronger. Recognising a past life partner can feel like meeting someone you have known for a very long time. The eyes, in particular, can look familiar, as the eyes are the windows to the soul. Sometimes you can meet someone for only a few moments, and you can feel as if you have known them for all your life; this is finding a past life partner. This is not the case if you are in a relationship that goes on for years and yet you never feel you are getting closer.

Some of the most interesting relationships can be while travelling or on holiday, when you have nothing else to lose and you are unguarded and open to the opportunity.

Problems arise when you do eventually manage to make a connection with a past life love, but for some reason the link is broken again. This can put you in a confused state, where you end up dreaming of the 'what ifs' for the rest of your life.

'We all want someone to love us.
How many of us do that for ourselves?'
Medium Glynn Edwards

Relationships are our greatest learning tool. The greatest lesson-givers are the relationships we feel the most energy and emotion for. Being in a past life connection relationship, even though it may have the symptoms of a relationship meant to be, may just be the right person for right now. What we search for in others is in ourselves, ready to give to another.

Finding answers

Any unresolved question you might have for someone can be asked through meditation. We are all linked; the universe is within us, so there is no question we can't answer. Cords of connection run though all of us like a web, so no one is ever lost to us. Make sure you are in a nice relaxed state for your meditation and visualise the person you want to talk to sitting down. Ask if you can join them: if they say 'no', do the exercise another time; if they say 'yes', have the conversation about whatever issue is unresolved. You might be surprised to find that what they say isn't what you expected at all.

How to control anxiety in relationships

1: It is better to want someone rather than need them, because when you want someone you are whole as a person. People like to be needed, but that will only keep both of you dependent and down. Learn to take care of yourself. That is when you can trust yourself. If you don't have self-trust you feel out of control, which leads to anxiety. Trust yourself that you can cope with whatever happens. It is an illusion to think safety comes from someone else.

2: We can control our anxiety by mixing our source of love, and I don't mean that in a physical sense; I mean it in the sense of not needing all our love from one person, but by having love with family and friends.

3: Reassure your inner child. People talk of the inner child as if that is the vulnerable side of our personality. Anyone who knows children will know how resilient they are. For example, if a child is lost in a shopping centre they will normally find someone to help them, plus a bag of sweets! So when reassuring your inner child, don't talk to yourself as if you are vulnerable, know you are strong but just need to be reassured that you can look after yourself.

4: Breathe. It's the best way to calm your anxiety. When taking a drag on a cigarette people breathe deeply, but it isn't the cigarette that calms nerves, it's that breath. When we're feeling anxious, our breathing shortens. So, being conscious of our breathing will take away some of the symptoms.

5: Have faith in yourself. We often have faith in something external to ourselves. We may say that we have faith in Spirit, or the universe or God, but very often we lack that faith in ourselves.Confidence we can fake, faith we can't, even though the two go hand in hand and one can lead the way to the other. We have God inside of each of us, and when we truly love, it is as if we look into the face of God in our lover's eyes.

The rules of manifestation

Choose what characteristics in a person's personality you want.

Know yourself. What do you need to be open to, or what are you willing to change? If you are not willing to compromise, you won't move forward.

Understand that the energy around you, your aura, will tell people things about you in an unconscious way. If you feel you need to protect yourself, your aura will stay close to your body. We see this all the time in other people, but do not realise what it is.

Know what you want, but take what shows up; trust the universe to know what you need isn't always what you want! If the feelings match how you want to feel, who cares what the person looks like!

When love seems impossible to find

The first question to ask yourself is, what are you looking for? Are you looking for a long-term investment only? If so, the energy that you will be sending out is sure to create the impression that you want to trap someone into a relationship. Follow these rules to make yourself more open to love:

1: Do not try to make an investment out of love. Give it its freedom. To invite love you must also invite hurt – to be open to one, you have to be open to the other.

2: Do not just look for a soul mate connection; you may need a connection in this lifetime to continue that connection into the next.

3: What turns you on? Make fantasies about fun and love as well as sex. Add green and pink to your energy field.

4: Carry a rose quartz crystal.

5: Cut the cords from old relationships. Do not expect an old relationship to be revived.

6: Light a candle to mark as a beacon for love. You can buy candles that have been made with the intent of finding love.

7: Love without long-term goals.

Cord cutting

When we make love with someone, or even sleep next to them, cords of attachment are formed between the two souls. It helps us find each other when we cross over. That's why when you are trying to get over someone you can still be pulled around emotionally by what they are doing in their life. It can be hard to cut these cords as through these cords flow love and energy. But we may need to cut them so we can welcome new love into our life.

The best way to cut those cords is through meditation and visualisation.

1: Take a large piece of paper and write down the names of everyone you feel you may still have an attachment to. Leave plenty of space between each name.
2: Take a pendulum, hold it over your hand and ask it which direction is yes, and then which direction is no. With that information, take the pendulum and dangle it over the names. Going from one name to the next, ask the question 'Do I still have cords attached to this person?'
3: The pendulum will answer yes or no. If the answer is no, cross that name off your list. If the answer is yes, close your eyes and visualise this person before you; you can see the cords running between you. However you see them is right for you. Give this person a kind thought, then with a large pair of scissors made from light cut away at these cords until they are all broken. If the cords don't break it may not be the right time for you to let go, so try this another time. When they do break, send a bit of healing love to yourself, and know that you have moved on. Intention is the key. New cords may form, but you always have the skills and tools to break them. You can do this with as many people as you like, including friends and family members.

In my own experience, I have thought I had moved on from a partner only to realise I hadn't whilst crying over a bowl of washing up. I noticed that the pain was in my solar plexus area. It felt like small spring onions being pulled out of my chest. I feel these were the cords of our attachment being removed. I have felt much better ever since.

Conclusion

Whatever you believe or dream you can do, start doing it now. Everything that ever has been or ever will be comes from our mind. If we believe we have strong psychic ability, we are tuning into the greatest tool we have. Believe it until it becomes so.

I remember the first time I agreed to do readings on a radio show. I had no idea if I could do it. I had done phone readings before, but I didn't know if nerves would get the better of me, or if I could handle the amount going on in the studio. Three factors made the difference:

- I had an inner knowing that I would be successful.
- I decided it didn't matter if it didn't work out, because I don't have an attachment to what others think of me – you should only look at yourself through your own eyes, not anyone else's. I was prepared to have a go and break past fear.
- Most importantly, I set out the intention to be in service to everything and everyone all of my life not in just this moment.

These are the three most important factors needed to bring forward a brilliant life as well as psychic excellence.

As psychics, we are spiritual in everything we do, not just when we are giving readings. That's not to say that we open the door to anyone who wants to take advantage of us. The kindest gift you can give someone can be your honesty, as long as you know that is your truth in the way you see the truth to be, but not the only truth.

To be in service to others is to be the most connected to yourself. Bring forward your light in as many rays and colours as you see in nature.

Shine brightly.

I wish you faith on your journey.

ACKNOWLEDGMENTS

Often we pass in and out of people's lives without knowing the difference we make to those people. Sometimes the people who challenge us the most can give us the best benefits, without us or them even knowing.

I couldn't begin to list all those people I have come into contact with who have inspired me into writing this book and who have aided me along this pathway. I am grateful for all the twists and turns in the road.

For those who have given me practical help, kindness and support (I won't name you, as you know who you are even when I do not), I thank you with all my heart. I am indebted to James Topping for giving me unbending belief, faith and words; Sebastian Strasburg for all the time he took to help with my English, which we discovered is my second language, my first being gobbeldy gook; and John Hunt at *O Books* for coming when 'cosmically ordered'.

Cheryl Van Blerk for her advice. Emma Reyes for being her wonderful self.

Mark Sherwood for his support in all my hair-brained schemes.

The College of Psychic Studies where I still continue to learn as I teach. Arthur Findlay College for excellent tutors and a wonderful setting.

PUBLICATION ACKNOWLEDGMENTS

Part two: Tuning into Spirit:
Balancing our core male and female energies – Alchemy of Voice By Stewart Pearce.
Mediumisistic communication and proof of life – Work sheets and information taught by collective tutors at Arthur Findlay College.
Helen Duncan – The story of Helen Duncan Materialization Medium By Alan E Crossley.
Seeing Oneness – Interview I had with Neale Donnald Walsch
Sixth Sense – Dr. Laurie Nadel

www.lightofspirit@gmail.com

Useful Contacts in the UK and America

Name: Mind Body Soul Online Resource
Summary: One of the UK's finest resources for all things relating to Mind, Body and Soul. The site includes a resource and location directory for many complementary and holistic therapies, spiritual awareness, personal development courses and health news.
Website: http://www.mbspages.co.uk/

Name: Mind Body Soul Exhibitions
Summary: This site, which is connected with the one above, has information on exhibitions in the UK that are concerned with complementary therapies, personal growth and spiritual awareness. Many of the exhibitions include lectures and workshops as well as having a large selection of therapies and products on offer. Free programmes for the exhibitions are usually available, either by download or by post, 2 months before the event takes place.
Website: http://www.mbsevents.co.uk/

Name: British Astrological and Psychic Society (BAPS)
Summary: Founded in 1976, BAPS offers workshops and accredited (and vetted) readers in a variety of fields including tarot, palmistry, astrology, numerology, healing, psychics, runes.
Website: http://www.baps.ws/

Name: Psychic Directory UK
Summary: A vast directory covering the British Isles.
Website: http://www.psychicdirectory.co.uk/

Name: Spiritualist Association of Great Britain
Summary: The stated purpose of this organisation is to 'offer evidence through Mediumship of the continuation of the personality after physical death, and to relieve suffering through spiritual healing'. They also offer courses, workshops, healing, events and services.
Website: http://www.sagb.org.uk/

Name: Arthur Findlay College
Summary: Located in Stansted and billed as 'the world's foremost college for the Advancement of Spiritualism and Psychic Sciences', the college (and residential centre) offers many courses, lectures and demonstrations.
Website: http://www.arthurfindlaycollege.org/

Name: College of Psychic Studies
Summary: The college, located in the heart of London, offers a huge variety of courses and workshops focusing on psychic development, personal and spiritual growth, trance, mediumship, meditation and healing.
Website: http://www.collegeofpsychicstudies.co.uk/

Name: Findhorn Press

Summary: A small publishing house based in northeast Scotland offering books, cards, CDs and DVDs on many mind, body and spirit topics such as self-help, psychic children, nature and ecology.

Website: http://www.findhornpress.com/HostedStore.LassoApp

Name: Cygnus Books

Summary: Offer a wide selection of mind, body and spirit books at discounted prices, many at 20-50% less than the published price. They also produce a free magazine, *The Cygnus Review.*

Website: http://www.cygnus-books.co.uk/

Name: The Institute of Spiritualist Mediums

Summary: Offers courses, events, seminars and workshops on mental, physical and trance mediumship. The ISM is 'intent on raising the standard of mediumship'.

Website: http://www.ism.org.uk/

Name: Society for Psychical Research

Summary: Founded in 1882 by a distinguished group of Cambridge scholars, the Society for Psychical Research was the first of its kind to examine allegedly paranormal phenomena in a scientific and unbiased way. Today the society continues with its aim of understanding events and abilities commonly described as 'psychic' or 'paranormal' by promoting and supporting important research in this area. Through the publication of scholarly reports and the organisation of educational activities, it acts as a forum for debate and promotes the dissemination of information about current developments in the field.

Website: http://www.spr.ac.uk/

Koestler Parapsychology Unit

Summary: The unit is part of the Psychology Department (School of Philosophy, Psychology and Language Sciences) at the University of

Edinburgh. It consists of a group of academic staff and postgraduate students with an active interest in parapsychology.
Website: (http://moebius.psy.ed.ac.uk/)

Name: Spiritualists' National Union
Summary: Noting that they are 'probably the largest Spiritualist organisation in the world', the SNU are 'the recognised national body in the United Kingdom for Spiritualism'. The website has a wealth of information and there is a list of registered and certified mediums and healers, churches and centres.
Website: http://www.snu.org.uk

Name: Psychic News Bookshop
Summary: A large selection of books on spiritualism, etc.
Website: http://www.psychicnewsbookshop.co.uk/

Name: Occultopedia
Summary: Wikipedia for the occult, with a link to the site's large occult shop (based in the USA). Brilliant for checking facts and information.
Website: http://www.occultopedia.com/occult.htm

Name: The Psychic Times
Summary: An online newspaper 'with up-to-the-minute news, articles, interviews and information on near death experiences, psychic phenomenon, paranormal activity, and proof of life after death'.
Website: http://www.thepsychictimes.com/

Name: Institute of Psychic Development
Summary: The Institute of Psychic Development is widely known for its skills in presenting psychic, extra sensory perception (ESP), telephony, developing mediumship, intuition, psychometry, chakra,

dowsing, sixth sense, aura, higher self, spirit guides, angels, past lives, akashic records, psychic healing, astral projection lessons and psychic courses in a clear and professional manner. There are home study psychic development courses suitable for the beginner to the advanced.
Website: http://www.psychicstudies.net/

Name: Psychic Artworks
Summary: The website of psychic artist June-Elleni Lane examining the 'visual representation of Energy that can only be perceived with the Psychic Senses' in all its various forms – automatic writing/drawing, energy art, icons, spirit portraiture, etc.
Website: http://www.psychicartworks.com/

Name: Esoteric Agents
Summary: Agents who represent esoterically-inclined experts for the fields of television, radio, books, etc. They also run correspondence courses in a number of subjects such as angels, Egyptian mysteries, palmistry, psychic development, tarot, witchcraft, etc.
Website: http://www.esoteric-e.co.uk/

Watkins Bookshop
Summary: One of the world's leading specialists in mysticism, occultism, Oriental religion, astrology, perennial wisdom and all aspects of contemporary spiritualism.
13 Cecil Court Leicester Square London
Website: http://www.watkinsbooks.com/

Magazines:

The Skeptic Magazine
Summary: *The Skeptic* is the UK's only regular magazine to take a sceptical look at pseudoscience and claims of the paranormal.

Founded in 1987 by Wendy Grossman, the magazine is now co-edited by Professor Chris French from the Anomalistic Psychology Research Unit, Goldsmiths College, London, and Victoria Hamilton. It is a non-profit magazine published four times a year, available only by subscription. An invaluable resource for journalists, teachers, psychologists and inquisitive people of all ages who yearn to discover the truth behind the many extraordinary claims of paranormal and unusual phenomena.
Website: http://www.skeptic.org.uk/

Spirit & Destiny
Summary: Ever wanted to free your mind, body and spirit and explore a new way to live your life? Well, now you can, simply by turning the pages of *Spirit & Destiny* magazine and embarking on a journey of self-discovery. Inside you'll find out all there is to know about the worlds of astrology, psychics and holistic therapy.
Website: (https://secure2.subscribeonline.co.uk/SPIR/index.cfm)

Fate and Fortune
Summary: *Fate & Fortune* is a guide to what the stars have in store for you over the following month. It is a classic mix of editorial including health, fashion and real life stories but everything is linked in some way to the planetary movements and psychic interest. *Fate & Fortune* gives the stargazer a light-hearted look into the future. It is read by those with an interest in the stars, new age themes and complementary/alternative health issues.
Website: (http://www.bauer.co.uk/website/fate.cfm)

It's Fate
Summary: Chat magazines - *It's Fate* is the accessible, practical, life-enhancing monthly psychic magazine for women, providing the most personal psychic advice and the most paranormal real life stories.
Website: (http://www.ipcmedia.com/magazines/chatitsfate)

Prediction Magazine
Summary: As a mystical guide to love, life and the future, *Prediction Magazine* is bursting with upbeat, fascinating features on psychic phenomena, love and spirituality. There are over 15 pages of essential horoscopes every month, combining expert knowledge with inspiring advice. Established in 1936, it's a trusted guide to all things esoteric.
Website: http://www.predictionmagazine.com/index.htm

Kindred Spirit
Summary: '…a myriad of information from events, workshops, complementary health, travel articles, new products and the most comprehensive A-Z of all things to improve both your well-being and your lifestyle…'
Website: (http://www.kindredspirit.co.uk/)

Fortean Times
Summary: *Fortean Times* is a monthly magazine of news, reviews and research on strange phenomena and experiences, curiosities, prodigies and portents.
Website: (http://www.forteantimes.com/)

Magazines in the USA:

Fate Magazine
Summary: Published continuously since 1948, *Fate* is the longest-running publication of its kind, supplying its loyal readership with a broad array of true accounts of the strange and unknown for nearly 60 years. From psychics and Spiritualists, archaeological hotspots and fringe science, to authoritative UFO and paranormal investigations, and readers' personal mystic experiences, *Fate* articles are factual, informative, and entertaining. *Fate's* unique mix serves the growing audience of people seeking both answers and entertainment.
Website: http://www.fatemag.com/

Awareness Magazine
Summary: A bi-monthly Holistic publication covering such issues as alternative health treatments, natural health products, fitness and personal growth, spirituality, the environment, and much more.
Website: http://www.awarenessmag.com/

The American Spirit newspaper
Summary: *The American Spirit* newspaper is an educational newspaper that has been published since 1992. The goal of the paper is to educate (bring out into the open) people about what is going on behind the scenes in all areas of their life, especially finances, the economy, spirituality, family, medicine, health issues, healing, etc.
Website: http://www.americanspiritnews.com

Web radio shows:
Hay house radio: http://www.hayhouseradio.com/
My Spirit radio: www.myspiritradio.com

Sceptic sites:
Association for Skeptical Enquiry
Website: (http://www.aske.org.uk/)

Bad Psychics
Website: (www.badpsychics.com)

RECOMMENDED READING

Author	Title	Comments
John Edward	Any of his books	American medium describing his life and his clients, good insights for new mediums.
Neale Donald Walsch	Any of his books. Esp. *Conversations with God* and *Tomorrow's God*	Opening spiritual awareness.
Wayne W Dyer	Any of his books. Esp. *The Power of Intention*	Inspirational .
Sonia Choquette	*Diary of a Psychic*	Good real life story.
Doreen Virtue	*The Light Workers Way*	Very good for budding psychics.
Judy Hall	*Psychic Protection*	A must for anyone healing or working with energy.
Jude Currivan	*The Wave, 8th Chakra*	*8th Chakra* is an explanation of what's happening towards 2012.
Gordon Smith	Any if you want to read up on mediumship	He is a great medium.
Will Storr	*Will Storr Vs The Supernatural*	Funny and interesting.
Stewart Pearce	*The Alchemy of Voice*	Great book on how to balance energy and find your voice. Excellent for people who want to talk for a living.
Candace Pert	Everything you need to know to	Candace is a scientist who has found ways to prove cosmic

	feel good	ordering. This is a must read!
Jerry and Esther Hicks	Ask AND IT IS GIVEN	Any of these channels of Abraham are brilliant at explaining the way our thoughts create our life.
Dr. Laurie Nadel's	Sixth Sense	Wonderful explanation of the mind.
Sue Allen	Spirit Release	Information you may need for some clients.

Other books by Becky Walsh:

West End Theatre Ghosts, co author Ian Shillito, published by Tempus.

SOME RECENT O BOOKS

Back to the Truth

5,000 years of Advaita

Dennis Waite

A wonderful book. Encyclopedic in nature, and destined to become a classic. **James Braha**

Absolutely brilliant...an ease of writing with a water-tight argument outlining the great universal truths. This book will become a modern classic. A milestone in the history of Advaita. **Paula Marvelly**

1905047614 500pp **£19.95 $29.95**

Beyond Photography

Encounters with orbs, angels and mysterious light forms

Katie Hall and John Pickering

The authors invite you to join them on a fascinating quest; a voyage of discovery into the nature of a phenomenon, manifestations of which are shown as being historical and global as well as contemporary and intently personal.

At journey's end you may find yourself a believer, a doubter or simply an intrigued wonderer... Whatever the outcome, the process of journeying is likely prove provocative and stimulating and - as with the mysterious images fleetingly captured by the authors' cameras - inspiring and potentially enlightening. **Brian Sibley**, author and broadcaster.

1905047908 272pp 50 b/w photos +8pp colour insert **£12.99 $24.95**

Don't Get MAD Get Wise

Why no one ever makes you angry, ever!

Mike George

There is a journey we all need to make, from anger, to peace, to

forgiveness. Anger always destroys, peace always restores, and forgiveness always heals. This explains the journey, the steps you can take to make it happen for you.
1905047827 160pp **£7.99 $14.95**

IF You Fall...

It's a new beginning

Karen Darke

Karen Darke's story is about the indomitability of spirit, from one of life's cruel vagaries of fortune to what is insight and inspiration. She has overcome the limitations of paralysis and discovered a life of challenge and adventure that many of us only dream about. It is all about the mind, the spirit and the desire that some of us find, but which all of us possess. **Joe Simpson,** mountaineer and author of *Touching the Void*
1905047886 240pp £9.99 $19.95

Love, Healing and Happiness

Spiritual wisdom for a post-secular era

Larry Culliford

This will become a classic book on spirituality. It is immensely practical and grounded. It mirrors the author's compassion and lays the foundation for a higher understanding of human suffering and hope. **Reinhard Kowalski** Consultant Clinical Psychologist
1905047916 304pp £10.99 $19.95

A Map to God

Awakening Spiritual Integrity

Susie Anthony

This describes an ancient hermetic pathway, representing a golden thread running through many traditions, which offers all we need to understand and do to actually become our best selves.
1846940443 260pp **£10.99 $21.95**

Punk Science

Inside the mind of God

Manjir Samanta-Laughton

Wow! Punk Science is an extraordinary journey from the microcosm of the atom to the macrocosm of the Universe and all stops in between. Manjir Samanta-Laughton's synthesis of cosmology and consciousness is sheer genius. It is elegant, simple and, as an added bonus, makes great reading. **Dr Bruce H. Lipton**, author of *The Biology of Belief*

1905047932 320pp **£12.95 $22.95**

Rosslyn Revealed

A secret library in stone

Alan Butler

Rosslyn Revealed gets to the bottom of the mystery of the chapel featured in the Da Vinci Code. The results of a lifetime of careful research and study demonstrate that truth really is stranger than fiction; a library of philosophical ideas and mystery rites, that were heresy in their time, have been disguised in the extraordinarily elaborate stone carvings.

1905047924 260pp b/w + colour illustrations **£19.95 $29.95** cl

The Way of Thomas

Nine Insights for Enlightened Living from the Secret Sayings of Jesus

John R. Mabry

What is the real story of early Christianity? Can we find a Jesus that is relevant as a spiritual guide for people today?

These and many other questions are addressed in this popular presentation of the teachings of this mystical Christian text. Includes a reader-friendly version of the gospel.

1846940303 196pp **£10.99 $19.95**

The Way Things Are

A Living Approach to Buddhism

Lama Ole Nydahl

An up-to-date and revised edition of a seminal work in the Diamond Way Buddhist tradition (three times the original length), that makes the timeless wisdom of Buddhism accessible to western audiences. Lama Ole has established more than 450 centres in 43 countries.

1846940427 240pp **£9.99 $19.95**

The 7 Ahas! of Highly Enlightened Souls

How to free yourself from ALL forms of stress

Mike George

7th printing

A very profound, self empowering book. Each page bursting with wisdom and insight. One you will need to read and reread over and over again! Paradigm Shift. I totally love this book, a wonderful nugget of inspiration. **PlanetStarz**

1903816319 128pp 190/135mm **£5.99 $11.95**

God Calling

A Devotional Diary

A. J. Russell

46th printing

"When supply seems to have failed, you must know that it has not done so. But you must look around to see what you can give away. Give away something." One of the best-selling devotional books of all time, with over 6 million copies sold.

1905047428 280pp 135/95mm **£7.99** cl.

US rights sold

The Goddess, the Grail and the Lodge

The Da Vinci code and the real origins of religion

Alan Butler

5th printing

This book rings through with the integrity of sharing time-honoured revelations. As a historical detective, following a golden thread from the great Megalithic cultures, Alan Butler vividly presents a compelling picture of the fight for life of a great secret and one that we simply can't afford to ignore. **Lynn Picknett & Clive Prince**

1903816696 360pp 230/152mm **£12.99 $19.95**

The Heart of Tantric Sex

A unique guide to love and sexual fulfilment

Diana Richardson

3rd printing

The art of keeping love fresh and new long after the honeymoon is over. Tantra for modern Western lovers adapted in a practical, refreshing and sympathetic way.

One of the most revolutionary books on sexuality ever written. **Ruth Ostrow**, News Ltd.

1903816378 256pp **£9.99 $14.95**

I Am With You

The best-selling modern inspirational classic

John Woolley

14th printing hardback

Will bring peace and consolation to all who read it. **Cardinal Cormac Murphy-O'Connor**

0853053413 280pp 150x100mm **£9.99** cl

4th printing paperback

1903816998 280pp 150/100mm **£6.99 $12.95**